ADRIENNE VON SPEYR

THE WORD

A Meditation on the Prologue to Saint John's Gospel

Translated by Alexander Dru

IGNATIUS PRESS   SAN FRANCISCO

Title of the German original:
First part (John 1:1) of the work
Johannes I: Das Wort Wird Fleish
Betrachtungen über das Johannesevangelium (1949, 2004)
© Johannes Verlag Einsiedeln and Freiburg
Published with ecclesiastical approval

Commentary on John 1:1–18 was
previously published by Collins in 1953 as
The Word: Meditation on the Prologue to John's Gospel.
Translated by Alexander Dru.
Reprinted with permission of Harper Collins Publishers, London.

Published in 1994 by Ignatius Press as part of
The Word Became Flesh: Meditations on John 1–5
© 1994 by Ignatius Press

Cover art:
Saint John

Evangelist, Byzantine miniature, 12th century
Biblioteca Marciana, Venice, Italy
© Scala/Art Resource, New York

Cover design by Roxanne Mei Lum

Published in 2019 by Ignatius Press, San Francisco
ISBN 978-1-62164-272-5
Library of Congress Control Number 2018949825
Printed in the United States of America ∞

CONTENTS

THE WORD IN THE BEGINNING: REVELATION

1:1. *In the beginning was the Word, and the Word was with God, and the Word was God.*

In the beginning was the Word. If the Word was in the beginning, then it was not the beginning, and the beginning was not the Word. For the Word was *in* the beginning. The beginning is the origin, the absolute beginning, the source, the Alpha; all beginning, origin as such, is utterly incomprehensible, intangible, colorless, timeless, forever beyond our grasp; it is that which always was. It is the divine and the fathomless in God. If there were anything corresponding to "becoming" in God, the beginning would be his eternal becoming. If there were growth or increase in God, the beginning would be his eternal increase. If there were darkness in God, the beginning would be his eternal darkness. But: *in the beginning was the Word*. The Word is expression, language, fulfillment, light. So that in God the beginning was ever reality, the origin was always being, his fathomless abyss was always light. In God there was never any contradiction between the beginning and the Word, for the Word was in the beginning, the beginning in the Word; *the Word was* not only *with God*; the Word itself was God: *the Word was God*.

Yet the beginning was not the Word, and the Word was not the beginning. Life as we know it is full of oppositions and contradictions; they are a condition of life. The life that originates in this world only subsequently becomes the

Word; for though the Word was implicit in life from the first, so that life might become what it already is, as the Word fulfilled it is born out of the beginning. For life in the world is doing and suffering; being and growth; light and darkness; foundation, end, and aim. But for oppositions and contradictions there would be no becoming, no movement, no growth, and consequently no life.

God is eternal life, and because he is eternal, there is no contradiction in him; it is wiped out eternally in his unity. But since, nevertheless, God is life, his life can only be conceived and pictured as the antithesis between the beginning and the Word. God manifests his life by bringing all contradictions and oppositions in the world to unity in himself, leading them up to his unity; for the life of God consists not only of his goodness and greatness and light but equally of his power over death and darkness, his authority over small things, his dominion over evil. We move from darkness into light, because in us the Word is not in the beginning. In God the Word is in the beginning; he is therefore eternal light, and there is no darkness in him.

In God, then, the beginning and the Word were present from the beginning. That is why the beginning contained the Word of God from the beginning. The Word, considered apart and in itself, is not the beginning; it is the very opposite of the beginning: it is the fulfillment. For the opposite of the beginning is not the end, but the fulfillment. Indeed, the Word is so essentially the fulfillment of the beginning that it is essentially the power to originate, to bring forth new beginnings, and in so doing, in the very act of fulfillment, it becomes the source and the beginning for us. Wherever the Word acts, there is a beginning, a completely fresh start behind which it is impossible to go and that can never be undone. Such is the fruitfulness and the glory of the Word of God that every Word spoken by him is spoken for all eternity. One can never say of God's Word that it was not uttered or that it remained without effect. His Word is power, and all things that were made were made by his Word and by him alone. And without his Word was made nothing that was made. His Word is not like the word of man, which can be set aside and disregarded. It is eternally active because it is eternal life. Whenever it touches something, it brings forth life. For it is the eternal Word, the absolute Word, independent of an answer. The Word of God sounds, though no one listens. It does not, as with men, call for a dialogue between equals. Where the Word of God is concerned, the hearer vanishes to nothing. Whether we receive it or not, it is creative: once spoken, the effect follows and demonstrates that the Word is the fulfillment.

The Word that fulfills is creative; the fount and source of origins has the beginning within it. It is indeed in the beginning. It has the beginning eternally behind it because it was eternally in the beginning. But equally it has the beginning eternally within it, for it has power over the beginning. It *is* in the beginning; it does not *become* the Word in the beginning. Regarded as the fulfillment, it bears the beginning within it like a seed. A word always means something; it is an indication, a pointer, a sign, and consequently an undertaking, a promise of something more. Not being the beginning, it has the beginning within it. It is the fruit as well as the seed of the beginning. All origins begin in the Word. The Word is never added subsequently to a beginning. There is no darkness that is not surrounded by its light. No becoming that does not find meaning, form, and mission in the Word, nor any being that might not have an ever-new beginning in the Word.

And because the Word has the beginning in it, nothing fulfilled in the Word is an end, just as nothing God says or reveals to us has an end without a beginning concealed within it as seed. On the contrary, it is always a new beginning. The unity of the beginning and the Word consists in their unendingness; both are open to increase without end. Where man awaits an end, the Word awaits him, the Word that was in the beginning and signifies a new beginning. Where man believes he has understood the Word in the fulfillment of it, he is seized by the Word as promise and led on to a new mission. Because no fulfillment is ever an end, he knows that he stands in the presence of God.

The *Word was with God* as the expression of the beginning and therefore as the form of divine revelation: the beginning expresses itself in the Word, and so the Word is in the beginning, ready and willing to be expressed, to be sent forth and taken back. The fact that the Word is expressed and sent forth is the fulfillment of the beginning, insofar as everything unexpressed is expressed and everything without form receives form in the Word. It is in the Word that the beginning receives color and tone, and God communicates himself in the Word. It is therefore in the Word that God can distinguish himself from himself and in that way communicate knowledge about himself. But since the beginning expresses itself in the Word, and since God sends forth the Word, the Word is simultaneously taken back into the beginning and into God. For the beginning finds its form and thus its fulfillment in the Word, and the Word fulfills itself in an equal degree from out of the beginning and back into the beginning: its going forth and its return are one, and neither is thinkable without the other.

As the beginning, God declares *that* he is. As the Word, he declares *who* he is. If God were known only as the beginning, the world would not know who he is. The beginning is the God to whom there is no access. He is the incommensurable—so far above us that we are not merely unable to conceive it, but also remain unmoved by its greatness.

We are men living in time, in a finite world, and only finite things mean anything to us. There is nothing in us open to pure infinity. The infinite is what we cannot imagine, and that is why it means nothing to us. It has none of the characteristics we know. It cannot be felt, cannot be measured, and, being incomprehensible, it does not awaken any demands in us. Of a God like that we should know only that beyond our horizon lay the infinite from which perhaps we derive—for after all, we and the things about us originate somewhere—but we should not be moved by longing to strive toward the unknown as to our aim and end. As long as we are not spoken to by his Word, we are unable to say a single word to him, for in that case we should be without the Word. Even if we had grasped that there was some relation between the foundation of the world and ourselves, we could still only give it names we had invented and a content such as already existed in the world. We should perhaps know that our life, not being eternal life, needed to be given form; we should try to draw up certain laws based on our own experience of life and on that of the human race so as to order this existence of ours on proper lines, and in doing so we should perhaps discover something corresponding to the natural law. But these limits and laws, expressing a "moral" of existence, though conceived against the background of an unattainable unknown, would consist solely of negatives, and they would not help us to decipher the silent unknown or bring it closer to us. It is only when the beginning has become Word for us that our relation to the unknown gives birth to a longing for God and thus to love, which transforms all laws into something positive. Only when the beginning expresses itself as Word are we able to learn to know God, not only as our fulfillment, but even as the divine beginning.

God never creates without the Word, and all things that were made were made by him in the Word. Nevertheless, God speaks to us in two ways in the Word. There is the silent Word of God in the happenings of the world and the events of our daily lives. When God takes away what a man holds dearest, he speaks to him in that event. It is a question addressed to him, or an answer. It is in fact a communication that fulfills its promise, for the Word of God is always both an action and an accomplished action. But mankind did not want to understand God's language in that form; men could not endure the silent Word; they wanted and always want explanations. They behave as they do because they are lacking in love, for love can interpret a silent communication equally well. God therefore parted with his Word, sent it into the world, and gave man the explicit Word. And when it appeared in the world, men were able to apprehend it; it could be heard and understood. The Word of God began to speak in the language of men, putting questions and giving answers; questions and answers that sound and echo from the beginning, spoken among men, audible and distinct.

This Word, which came from God, which was sent forth by God, answered all the questions that man could ask God and withheld no answer that God could give man: these answers are given in all that the Word said on earth, in all that is deposited in Scripture, and in all that was instituted, so that the whole relationship between God and man is expressed in the Church and the sacraments. The explicit Word made man, too, was in the beginning, contained in God from the first. And just as Jesus Christ, the Word made flesh, is in every word of the creation and of the order of salvation, being the very foundation and aim of everything unexpressed and hidden, so, too, are the Church and the sacraments. They, too, are present in the unexpressed Word of God, contained in the Word from the beginning, because while not yet instituted and still unexpressed, formless, and to us unimaginable, they are already contained therein and themselves contain that which constitutes the fullness of the love of God. Both the sacraments and the Church were in the beginning, as they now exist, as his love, foreseen in every detail. They are, therefore, unexpressed but most really present in the opening verses of John's Prologue.

The Word spoke as that which it is: as the Word that was in the beginning. It makes known to us the beginning, that beginning which was before us, which is always before us, however far back we may go to reach firm ground—and by making the beginning known to us, it enables us to realize that, in relation to the Word, we ourselves are only a beginning and can never be anything else. No one who has heard the Word of God can say *more* of himself than that he is at the beginning. No one, though he has taken a thousand steps, can ever say that he has put even one step behind him and need not take the first step. Beginning is the form of the Christian life.

To be a Christian means to promise; it is a ceaseless undertaking that, as such, is never fulfilled; it means striving, seeking, struggling, straining, longing, knocking at the door; it is something always opening without ever being open, always unfolding and always trying to escape from the human center, which it can no longer endure. Within this ceaseless growth is the circle of joy and suffering, the one within the other, neither conceivable without the other—and not merely balancing and neutralizing each other (for in that case they would not be Christian)—but both present simultaneously, linked one within the other, in such a way that each and every suffering has its joy within it, or gives birth to joy, and every joy its suffering (just as a mother's joy over her child is concealed in her pains, and concealed in that joy is the suffering the child will subsequently cause her, and in that suffering again the joy of having suffered for it, each eternally dovetailed into the other). Joy and suffering are the one indivisible form of this ceaselessly expanding life, which consists in being burst open, that is, of life unfolding in the beginning.

It is the Word that breaks into man's life in this way. The Word always says something that "becomes"; it promises a truth that is never fulfilled because the truth is always richer than any finite fulfillment. It is a promise that is never kept to the end because it always leads and promises to lead to new possibilities beyond the reality known to us. When first the Word enters into a man, his whole being is shaken to its depths, his heart is set on fire, and he is tempted to turn his inmost self outward and lift it toward the Word. Then even what is told us about the beginning we can never grasp arouses a great longing in us. Word and fire are one, and we are drawn to the flame to be utterly consumed. The Word and the demand are one, and understanding the Word, we take everything upon ourselves in order to fulfill its demand. But each time we promise to fulfill the demand and keep the Word, each time we take a step to meet the Word and try to love, when we spread what we have before him, turning our inmost self outward so as to make a gift of it, we at once become cold again, tepid again, and once again we are at the beginning; for only the eternal Word contains within itself completed action, whereas we never do.

In this sense, the revelation of the Word always makes too great a demand upon the creature. At first the Word that God addresses to us looks harmless, like a human word. But instantly the fire within it begins to stir, insatiably embracing everything, demanding everything, consuming everything. At first the Word of God appears to be a word one can answer; it seems as though the balance between speech and reply could be maintained. But as one begins to understand that the Divine Word is eternally in the beginning, it becomes more and more clear that man's starting point never reaches the point of beginning and falls farther and farther behind. Skill and art of a human kind can always be learned, even though the purpose of the first lessons may not be clear. But gradually we acquire confidence, survey the subject as a whole, and with practice learn to master it. In learning the language and the art of God, in contrast, our view of the whole progressively diminishes. All our supports are wrested from us, and what remains are an ever-deeper insight into our failure and an increasing longing. We lapse farther and farther into the beginning.

All human accomplishments develop in an orderly manner according to some method or following some plan. Anyone wishing to learn a foreign language adopts a definite method. We imagine we can approach the Word of God in the same way and grow perfect in relation to him. But as often as our plan in relation to God seems to us to be bordering on the maximum, it turns out to be the minimum from God's point of view, a method that has not even grasped the first Word of God's language. Our own program will call for the performance of a maximum of devotions, but a minimum of real devotion. We confuse devotions and devotion, offering God the former in order to withhold the latter. Our whole performance before God is a pharisaical program, the center of which is our own perfection, with the result that it is blind to the Word spoken to us, the ever-new and ever-unexpected Word. The whole of man's progress consists in the perpetual destruction of the human center, thus making way for the ever-new beginning in which is heard the Word. For the Word alone leads to God and to the beginning. Man can be led to the beginning only if he himself is in the beginning. The only way to love is to overcome one's own point of view.

Man lives in three stages: beginning, center, and fire. But since man has no center in himself and may not have one, he is led by the Word into the fire, so that he may come to the beginning, which is God. Beginning and fire are one.

THE WORD IN GOD

1:2. *He was in the beginning with God.*

The eternal Word is never the beginning, the origin. It is born eternally of the beginning. The beginning is Father; the Word is Son. But *in the beginning was the Word*, and because the Son is in the Father, the Word is not a continuation proceeding from the beginning, and the Son is not a continuation proceeding from the Father. Being the Father's Word, the Son is a fresh beginning, because the eternal Father is eternally the same, and the Son cannot have a being different from the Father's. Yet the Son is not the Father, for the Word was *with* God.

And this indicates a distinction. God and the Word are not the same. What God is cannot be said: he is everything, the fullness, the origin, the beginning of everything. It is he who gives everything, and the Son is he who has everything, because everything is given him by the Father. It is the Father who possesses all love and gives it to the Son, and the Son is he who receives all love and so desires to lavish love on others, because he has received it in such abundance. This river of love is the common life of Father and Son; it is their "being together" and nothing else. It is as though two figures stood facing each other and the entire space between them were filled with love, a love that leaves each person his being, his contours, his form and appearance. But "being together" in this way does not suffice for the fulfillment of their love. So the Gospel goes on to say: *And the Word was God.* Suddenly, the Son appears in the Father. In their essence, both are one, and their love, too, is one, and with that the circle seems to be closed. But here, at the point where the end seems to be fulfilled, the Evangelist begins again with the first sentence: *He was in the beginning with God.* For the love between Father and Son is not a closed circle; on the contrary, it is the source of a new beginning.

This new beginning is the third in God, the Holy Spirit. He is the breath common to their love, the eternal meeting between Father and Son, the source of eternal life in God, which transforms their every joint fulfillment into a beginning, and, therefore, like the Father and the Son, he is source and origin, the beginning and the source of beginning. The Holy Spirit is the eternal unity of those who meet eternally in love. Because the Son is eternally face to face with the Father, the Word is with God, but since he is eternally in the Father, the Word itself is God. Because they are one, and the Spirit is their unity, their single love shines eternally. But nevertheless, and for that very reason, they are able to separate in the Son's earthly mission, in order to give the outpouring of their love new possibilities and add fresh perfections to their already perfect love.

God in his essence is Trinity. It is impossible that he should be only Father and Son. To be two means, in the long run, death. One and one, face to face forever, leads ultimately to the exhaustion of love. A third is always necessary to keep the love between two alive, a third that reaches out beyond the two who love each other. A task that fills and occupies them, a spring that feeds their love, a common interest, something or other to stimulate them, that leads them on, that makes a breach in the circle, an occasion for the eternal renewal of their love. Something that touches both of them and in that way keeps the relationship alive. Thus the Holy Spirit in God is really the source of eternal life, and for that reason he is all that is most inconceivable in God, so ethereal, so full of movement that to find a symbol for him is virtually impossible. He is the eternal superabundance, that which is ever more, ever greater—the fountain of life. That is why everything living is three, participates in the three, and must be taken up and plunged into the trinitarian life if it is to live.

God in his essence is Trinity. It is not true to say that the Father comes first, that the Son then comes into being, and that finally the Spirit proceeds from the relation between them; and consequently that God's love is merely the result of the relation between Persons, that the essence of God comes before the Persons, and the Persons before their love. The essence of God, rather, is trinitarian and consists essentially in love. For love is the essence that the Persons have in common. They do not *possess* love; they are love; they are bathed in a single, common love, a love that is common to them as is the unity of the Divine Being. Each Person loves the others with the same identical love with which they are loved. God is not a lover; God is love, and this love has a threefold form.

God in his essence is Trinity. He cannot, therefore, reveal himself otherwise than as trinitarian. Revelation itself is always something living, something personal, and must in consequence be trinitarian. The fact that God can reveal himself to the world, and desires to do so, implies a living unity between God and the world that has its ground in the living unity of the Spirit of Father and Son. In revealing himself, God emerges from his silence and beginning and is revealed to us in the Word. But the fact that he not merely speaks but also is understood and received by us is the work of the Holy Spirit, the source of all living unity. The whole of God's revelation is therefore trinitarian, and the good tidings tell of nothing but the Trinity. From one end of the Gospel to the other, the sole content of the Word of God is the Trinity, which is also the sole content of the creation.

Man himself bears the stamp and seal of the trinitarian life, for his life has a beginning or origin, a middle or center, and is consumed. But this parallel implies no similarity with eternal life; for man's beginning is birth out of nothing, and he never escapes from this origin. The center is persistence in being himself, flight from his beginning, and dread of his end. As his life burns out and dies, he is consumed: a descent, not a completion. God is eternal life in being; man's is a transitory life in nothing. That is why man craves for the safe center, the center where the memory of his origin does not haunt him and the thought of being consumed does not torture him. And for that very reason, his craving contradicts the essence of life. That center is the transition between the arrested movement of his beginning and consuming fire. A center, that is to say, hostile to the eternal life of God; and in order to raise it up to eternal life, the Word appeared in human form. The Word taught man in a human way—and, indeed, gave him the power—to convert beginning, center, and consummation into life within the eternal trinitarian life. In that life, man no longer hates his origin but together with the Word is eternally in the beginning, and this because he no longer shrinks from offering himself to the fire that presses upon the center and begins instead to understand surrender and sacrifice as eternal fruitfulness. Man tries to imprison his life within himself; that is why it is benumbed and dies. Christ allows his life to stream forth in his death, which is why he is eternal life, in which the fire leads back eternally to the beginning, bearing with it a new and living beginning. God is therefore only a complete circle in the sense of being completely open; with him the return to the beginning is an eternal progress to the ever new and unexpected. For in the Son's return to the Father is revealed the altogether unexpected: the Holy Spirit—for that very reason the demonstration of the absolute fruitfulness of love.

Thus even created man, in his essence, is a revelation of the trinitarian God. God creates in him a beginning, and, if he so wished, man could live this origin and existence of his in such a way that it lay in the eternal beginning of the Father. Further, God gives man clarity, that is to say, separates and distinguishes what is in man in order to give him the possibility of thinking and conceiving, but also in order to move him to love in the spirit, a love that leads to a new and richer unity: to the unity of man with himself, which presupposes the unity of man with God. And what is here said of the beginning (or existence), of the center (or attitude), and of his being consumed (or love) can be repeated in a thousand declensions of the whole creation: everything in creation is a mirror of the living God, and the mysteries of the created world of which we can never reach a simple understanding reflect the greater mysteries of the trinitarian life.

The human spirit, too, taken in itself, is threefold: it can hear God's Word and his questions, can receive and understand them, and finally can answer them. But since the individual who thus hears, understands, and answers is already open toward the outside, the trinitarian image is repeated more impressively in the relation between man and woman. As persons, they are independent, though woman derives from man. Their personal and reciprocal devotion manifests, primarily, the fulfillment of their twofold unity, just as at first only the love between Father and

Son appears in God. But in the same way (for everything is a simile) that the indescribable fruitfulness of eternal love reveals itself, in the Son's return to the Father, as a new beginning—that is, as the Holy Spirit—so, too, the child appears between man and woman. For it is the child who enables the love between man and woman to become eternal movement, transforms the seemingly complete into a true beginning and bursts open the circle that threatened to close—and it is also the child who reveals the supernatural character of love as grace by pointing to its divine origin (for the child is a gift of God). And contrariwise, the Holy Spirit flows out from God upon the world at the moment when the distance separating Father and Son has been widened to embrace the whole world.

Since man's created nature bears the seal and impress of the Trinity in its being, its spirit, and its love, he can only understand himself and live rightly if he understands himself and lives through the Trinity. He does so when he transposes his being and beginning into the eternal (and therefore ever new) beginning of God, when he abandons his center to the Son of God instead of to his own spirit, and when he allows himself to be consumed in the flame of the Holy Spirit's love.

In her openness toward God, the Mother of God herself is an image of the Trinity: in her expectation, in her consent, in her fulfillment. The whole Church is trinitarian in her structure: the Church that bestows eternal life in the sacraments and the Church that receives eternal life through them, eternal life, which is one in bestowal and reception. It is the divine life communicated to him by Christ through the Church that enables man to experience the eternal beginning in God and to make it the form of his creaturely beginning. Man's life then gradually ceases to be intelligible as something closed and rounded off; it gradually opens to new and undreamed-of possibilities, for everything God does to him marks a beginning and becomes more and more of a source. Before she conceived, Mary seemed perfectly open to God, and the Incarnation seemed to mark the limit of her possibilities. But, in fact, these were infinitely expanded: she became Virgin and Mother simultaneously and fulfilled the being of woman beyond all expectation. Moreover, the birth of the Son did not limit her vocation as Mother, but sowed a beginning beyond all hope, her call to universal motherhood. And at the very point where her end appeared certain, as one sees her bowed and moving away from the Cross, once again the conclusion, all human evidence to the contrary, was surpassed in the inconceivable beginning of eternal life in the Resurrection.

The life of God is always incalculable; nothing happens as we expect, and the fulfillment is infinitely richer than anything that might have been deduced from what was. Thus the end, humanly speaking, the human limit, death, is the place marked out for the emergence of eternal life: because it is there that the unending greatness of the divine beginning comes to light.

Man's origin, taken in itself, is unalloyed unhappiness; at the very best, his life is spent treading water in the despair of not getting farther, in the realization through experience that his whole existence runs away to nothingness if he fails to escape from his beginning. But if the Trinity stoops down to him, then man's origin becomes the point at which his divine origin reveals itself, and what was unhappiness becomes pure happiness in the knowledge of the love of God, who from now on grows greater and greater in our sight.

THE WORD AS CREATOR

1:3. *All things were made through him, and without him was not anything made that was made.*

The Word is in the beginning, and consequently all creation emanates from the Word. The origin of the world, too, is in the Word, and nothing that begins in the world begins outside the Word.

In God, in the Trinity, the Word is the meaning, the form, the impress, the expression, the clarity of Divine Being. It is through the Word that God reveals himself and in the Word that he can be grasped. The revelation of God is consummated in the Word. As the Word of revelation, the Word is in the first place a foreboding; it is the model and design of the meaning that already exists but that only receives adequate expression in the Word. The expression of the meaning in the Word does not alter the meaning, as such; it adds nothing to the meaning; it simply raises what was already there into the light. And yet the meaning is only fully grasped in the Word, fully converted into reality. The Word is both the image of meaning as well as its fulfillment.

Since the world is an expression and an image of God, its essence and foundations are rooted in the Word. Its inmost essence rests upon the Word and is only intelligible as the Word. The creature's relation to God is given to us in the essence of speech: it consists in question, deliberation, and answer. There is God's question, in the Word, to the creature; there is the creature's deliberation on the Word of God received; and there is the creature's answer to God in the Word. Such is the creature's nature, and it is not in his power to change it; it does not fall within the sphere of his free choice; on the contrary, prior to the realm of choice and to the sphere of our vacillation and irresolution lies the sphere that does not fall within the orbit of our freedom and that we cannot disturb. That basis is our nature grounded in God, and it is unaffected by our vacillating utterances. It is only above and beyond this foundation that we enter the sphere of hesitation, the sphere in which the Word of God may be heard or not heard, received or not received, answered or not answered. Only there can the relation between God and man become a dialogue or fail as a dialogue. Though even if man remains silent and refuses to hear the Word on this level, that does not alter the fact that the ground of his being, the unalterable character of the creature, whether he wills it or not, is involved in a dialogue with God. Ultimately even silence is a form and an expression of the Word, because the Word is in the beginning, and everything is created in the Word.

Indeed the articulate, spoken Word is not the only one; there is equally the *inner Word*: the consciousness, the knowledge, and the thought of spirit present to itself and capable of self-expression. Even in the creation of the world, the Word of God is not, in the first instance, expressed, uttered, or separated from the Father, but is in the Father; it is indistinguishable and unseparated from him; the creative Word is only revealed as different from the Father in Christ. And yet it is in God from the first as the Word in which everything is made. And correspondingly, everything in man is created through the Word; everything alive, everything spiritual rests on the Word, even though it is not the articulate Word. It is only in the Word that man awakens to himself. That is why silence is rooted in the Word and is part of the Word.

Much that people who love one another do not express is essentially word nevertheless. And every word spoken in God, whether it is the Word of God or the word of man, is really and essentially spoken, though it need not be articulate. God and man do not remain imprisoned within themselves in silence; it is not as though conversation were superfluous because everything were known. The dialogue is so essential and profound that simply being together fulfills the role of speech. It becomes superfluous for the Word to be conscious, articulate, and felt. Mutual contemplation is a dialogue. When a man who believes and loves God sees him as he appears, or is expressed or represented in the world, for example, in two people who love each other or in something beautiful or in suffering or whatever it may be that reveals the love of God, his looking at the object is a direct, immediate conversation.

True contemplation is the opposite of Quietism. True contemplation is a living flame, life bursting forth, a confession of faith. Contemplation is the living Word of God in the creation that burns in the substance of man like a hidden fire. Once God has spoken, once a soul has heard him, then silence is never again an empty silence, a mere reechoing of the Word, but a form of answer, a way of receiving the Word, indeed, its vital, active acceptance. In silence, the soul becomes the womb of the Word. Silence is the prelude to the dialogue and its continuation. In silence, a man who has heard the Word becomes a different man. Even though he has not fully understood the Word, it lives in him, it touches him, it works vitally in him and joins itself to this particular personal soul as the personal Word. The Word preached in the same way to a thousand souls is received differently and uniquely by each one of them in silence.

The whole creation, therefore, and each individual creature rest on the Word, are grounded in the Word, are founded in the Word, and unfold in the Word. The Word in the creation is threefold: there is man's word, the word of the Father's creature; there is the Word of Christ, the Son made Man; there is the word of the Christian baptized in the Holy Spirit. These three forms of the Word in creation are always one, which was in the beginning with God. For the Word in creation was in the beginning with God.

Man's original word, his first babbling as an infant, is pure; it is a word that is with God and deposited in God. Until desire and selfishness awaken to disturb the dialogue with God and convert the purity of the word into lies, the child's first words are in God and with God. It is immediate love. And man's last words, the last sigh in which he resigns himself, in which he lays his selfishness and his lies aside and turns back to God, is once again pure, because it is spoken in God. It is a return to the first stammerings of infancy. Once again it is a word of pure love. Both are words spoken in weakness, helpless before the love of God. The child has not yet discovered itself; the dying man has forgotten himself again. Between the two lies that duration which we call "our life", in which man draws away from God to lead a life of his own, no longer speaks in God but tries to speak on his own. Words of this kind are lies so long as we claim them as our own, as though they were our own work, our own creation. We drive ourselves out of paradise and exile ourselves from life with God. We harden ourselves and no longer want to hear the Word of God, out of which everything is created and without which nothing is made. Paradise is not the unself-consciousness of infancy; consciousness as such is in no sense remote from God. Paradise is life in God, and that is possible to the self-conscious spirit.

But it is only possible through Christ. It is only possible because the curve of man's life, which begins in God, sweeps away from God and returns to God in death, is enclosed within the curve of the Word made man, which runs its pure course in God, from the birth of the Lord to his death. For even in his separation from the Father during his life on earth, Christ is the Father's Word, born in his lap, doing nothing but what he sees the Father do. He continued to be the Word that was in the beginning and was in God.

This possibility, the power to be in God despite the separation that our creatureliness involves, is the Son's gift to the Christian in the Holy Spirit and through the sacraments. The babbling of the baptized infant is truly and really the Word of God; it lives in God and is spoken in God. And the Christian's every word lives in God and is deposited in God to the same degree in which he allows the Word of God to live in him. This fact, the fact that the Christian's word is deposited with God, is the fact of *prayer*. Prayer is this deposition of the word with God and its recognition by man.

Prayer is not, primarily, a word addressed by man to God, but a gift God has made to man through the Word. God gives us prayer; it is not we who give it to him. That is why it remains with God even in the creation. Man's word is only with God when it is deposited with God, that is to say, when his word corresponds to the Word of God, when he says what God wishes to hear. God does not desire man's self-made word; he does not want man to "express himself". Man should not suppose that God depends upon him and wishes to be informed about him. What God wishes to hear is simply the answer to his Word. Naturally the whole person may, and even should, be contained in the answer, but the whole person interests God only insofar as it is the answer to his Word. When two people who love each other correspond by letter, they can write all they please about themselves, provided it does not become a sort of informative monologue about their own particular I. In that case, their monologue would be dead, and the Word would never come to life in the one who receives it.

Prayer, then, is a gift that God makes to us in his Word. In it, he gives us the possibility of hearing as well as of saying, of seeking as well as of finding, and thus of leading a life of the spirit in God, of taking part in the life of the living God. In doing this, he really uses his Word for our own. And so in prayer, we can give him back the Word he has given us as our own; he receives it from us as ours. But it nevertheless remains the Word of God, which was in the beginning with God and remains deposited in God. And in this, there is a threefold meaning.

The answer we give God is only an answer when it is a word accepted and received back by God. That is the only sense in which man's word is valid for God. If a complete stranger comes up to me while I am working and interrupts me with the request to be allowed to share in my work and be initiated into it, that would not imply any obligation on my part to comply with the request. I should have no occasion to entertain his suggestion. Only an already existing relationship to the stranger could influence me to fall in with his request. In the same way, the fact that we speak to God implies an already existing relationship, established and recognized by God; it implies that God is willing to listen and has inclined himself to the word of man in the Word of God. For it is only when God speaks to man that he inclines toward him and is ready to

accept and use him. Man's word begins to be a dialogue
with God when God listens to him. But just as he loved
us before we began to love him, so he heard us before we
began speaking to him. The word of man, as such, never
reaches the ear of God. He finds us before we have looked
for him and hears us before we have spoken to him. Our
words are a secondary matter compared with his attention. Prayer is more a matter of God's listening than of
our speaking. Prayer is good if it catches God's attention,
not when it seems well expressed in our eyes. A sigh may
well reach the ear of God when years of beautiful prayers
fail to do so.

Secondly, because prayer is a gift of God, it can never
remain within the individual. It always reaches out beyond
the individual. Since the Word of God is a living, creative source, prayer is given to man so that he may hand it
on, and, what is more, in two ways: he must impart it to
others and pray for others. He must impart it to those for
whom he prays, and he is in duty bound to pray for those
to whom he imparts it. That is why prayer is both individual and social.

Thirdly, the unspoken word is no less essentially part of
a true conversation than what is said. Words are supported
on the unexpressed foundation of a common understanding in love. This foundation is the reciprocal, the essential, the absolute Word. It does not need to be expressed;
rather, it assigns all the relative and explicit words their
place and expresses itself in them. In prayer, this unspoken word of love is deposited in the grace of God. When
a man uses a particular form of words to God and says
he will love him above all things, it is probably untrue as
among relative words, since he still loves the world and
does not live exclusively for God. Yet God accepts the
words in grace, accepts them for what he has already given

the man, as a fully affirmative Yes; God hears the word in all the fullness in which it is deposited in him. Somehow or other it is also *our* word, for it is after all we who utter it, but it belongs far more to God than to us because it is left to him, deposited with him. Being given to God, it becomes his word, and, at the same time, it takes on the color of its surroundings and is transformed by grace into the Word of God. But it does not cease to be a dialogue, for it is a Word of love. When we say Yes to God, the affirmation is ours, but since it was given to us by him and deposited with him, it belongs to him far more than to us. We do not say it of ourselves, by ourselves, or in ourselves. We have no rights upon it. In the Gospel story, the son who said No but did his father's will uttered the Yes of real assent, though his relative, human word was No. His Yes was deposited in God; it was not a word that belonged to him. Of course, the word deposited with God must correspond to the word we say to him; but as ultimately we are unfit to dispose of our own Yes, we must give it to God in prayer so as not to live in ourselves but in his Word, the Word in which we are created.

Ultimately everyone is confronted with his word as deposited in God. The deposited word is God's image of each particular man, present in him from the beginning. And then it will be seen whether the individual corresponds to the thought of God or not. He will not be able to do so except through the grace of the Word of God made man, purified, burst open, and expanded by purgatorial fire to the breadth and the fullness of his word deposited in God. There, in fire, he will lay aside his irresolution and his vacillation and conform to God's thought; he will have to learn to love through the painful expansion of love until he becomes one with his word deposited in God.

THE WORD AS LIFE

1:4a. *In him was life.*

The life that is in the Word of God is not the biological life we know. It is not the teeming, endlessly diversified, individualized, striving, swarming life that grows and dies down again. It is not the life that lives warding off death. The life that we know is the opposite of death and needs death in order to renew itself. The life that is in God is eternal life. We simply cannot conceive it; because of its nature, eternal life defies conception. Our notions and concepts bind and define, while eternal life is boundless and free and makes nonsense of our definitions. If all else in God could be described, eternal life would still be indescribable. We can of course use images and comparisons in an attempt to illuminate the fullness of life in God: fruitfulness that multiplies itself, a spring that flows out to become a sea, the storm that carries everything before it. But they are only commonplaces and fail to express what eternal life is. Earthly, animal, and even spiritual life can be grasped indirectly, because it has a limit, an outer shell, a body, a form of expression; the outer form enables us to experience life even though it defies conception. But in God there is no limit, no outer shell, so that what passes conception in him remains utterly incomprehensible.

The life of this world can be imagined only as movement, as becoming, as striving toward being. The divine life, in contrast, is the fullness of life and consequently perfect peace, power, and authority, the absolute affirmation of being and becoming. We measure all things by our own unrest and fickleness and find therein the quintessence of vitality. Where God demands *being*, we think only of *becoming*. Where he waits for us to join him in giving his eternal confirmation to being, we at the very best affirm our becoming, the unrest in our hearts. For us the quintessence of delight is movement; if we are not moving ourselves, then at least we want something about us to move in order that we may enjoy change—if it is only warmth that penetrates us, a breeze that cools us, or the waves of the sea that delight us. From change in us and around us we expect progress, since to us the very essence of life is development. What lies behind us we regard as lower; what lies before us as higher. We understand life as constant endeavor. But the poverty and need that are at the source of our striving are altogether foreign to eternal life. Life for us is an anxious affair, and we snatch what we can, whereas eternal life is free and open, all giving and receiving, accepting and granting, an undisturbed flow of riches; eternal life is love. What we strive for can never be a condition; it is only a movement striving for something better. This profound unrest is attached deep down in us to our sins and to the consequences of sin. To that extent, it is the opposite of life; it is want and the proximity of death. Neither can we overcome the death in us by augmenting what we call life; we can do so only by giving our assent to the eternal life of God.

That is the life to which we ought to cling and assent with our deepest self. The Yes our lips say to God must correspond to the Yes that is deposited in God. In God, the word is the expression of life, and the Word God has given us must correspond and answer to that life. We can only give him this corresponding answer when we have somehow or other understood, or begun to understand, that he is life. When we have begun to understand, however dimly, that without him we are dead. That the life we lead without him is a dead life, though the death in which we tarry will always look like life to us. Only when we begin to feel dimly that we are really dead without him can we begin to see dimly that he is *life* and thus our life, too. The more we feel our want, and the emptier we know ourselves to be, the more receptive we become to eternal life, which is always giving itself to us.

Usually, we think of eternal life as a distant self-contained world, rounded like a sphere, in which—at any rate for the moment—we have no part. But the more we open ourselves in our poverty, the more open and accessible eternal life seems to us: it becomes an unending source of strength that comes to us and inundates us and so overwhelms us that it spells certain death to our dead and tepid lives.

When a man reflects on the words *in him was life*, he tends to imagine he knows something about that life theoretically, something about God, the principle of life, from which the different forms of life in the world derive and by which they are sustained; he thinks of this principle as the source of worldly life. But the more he thinks about it and tries to grasp it conceptually, the more lifeless and desiccated his imagined possession becomes. He is like a man in possession of an explosive he knows all about; he can calculate its effects and teach others about it. But once it explodes, once his knowledge is put into practice and the reality of eternal life draws near, it blows all his calculations sky high, and him, too. If God really shows him what life is, if he lets him see the merest corner of its glory, he is bowled over and flung to the ground by the power that surpasses all things. He will have no more use for notions and concepts, those little cups into which he thought to pour the sea. That is what happens to those who find Jesus Christ in faith: the example of eternal life he gives us, which he himself is, is so overwhelming that no one who has seen it in faith can ever again think of becoming like him. From then on, the imitation of the life of God can mean only one thing: it consists in allowing oneself to be inundated by his life; and the contemplation of the life of God consists in closing one's eyes, as in shame, at such a superabundance of life.

The life of God is *unique* life. That is why all life created by him is, in its way, singular and unique. But the uniqueness of God signifies inexhaustible riches. His uniqueness embraces every kind of variety and difference: it is greater than number and more than quality. The life of God manifests itself in millions of forms, all of which are unique. God is always the same and yet never the same. He is so unique that every time he reveals himself his revelation is unique. He is the opposite of all one can accustom oneself to. And because he is the one, the unique, embracing every possibility within his uniqueness, he can therefore accept and receive back the millionfold Yes of his creatures. It is only in the unity of his assent that the creatures' assent is really an affirmation of life. He is perfect and complete; we are barely indicated; he is what he is, whereas we can never get to the bottom of our existence and essence. It always remains unintelligible to us, something fugitive and dissolving we cannot grasp, and the more we snatch at it, the more we concern ourselves with our being and our self, the farther it eludes our grasp. The more we try to analyze and unravel it, the more it frays to pieces in our hands. It is only when we give all that is incomprehensible in our lives back to the clear unity of God's life that we can live and our life ceases to be a problem. And a ray of God's uniqueness enters our life: as a result of his love, it receives a weight and a significance that is valid in eternity. We are always unnecessary to the life of God. But the very fact of being superfluous offers us a way of entering into an understanding of his superfluity.

It is when we forget ourselves and rise above ourselves that we discover God's grace. In grace, our I is no longer a problem, and there is consequently no problem over the apprehension of God. God does not wish us to analyze and conceive him as we do an earthly object. He shows us enough of himself to fill us, unite us, clarify us: and as long as man is content with what God gives him of his life, he lives in God and upon God and all is as it should be. It is only when a man begins to count up what God has given him and is on the lookout for more, when he tries to conceive and understand the life in God he has been given and tries to go beyond it in an attempt to get beyond the mystery of eternal life, that he is precipitated out of life. Then he realizes that he is only a part, a piece, a fragment. Had he remained in grace, he would have possessed eternal life—so abundantly that he could have swum and plunged about in it for all eternity. But man can possess grace only if he abandons himself to it confidently. He can only find the unity of God for which he is looking, and his own unity after which he is striving, by perpetually giving himself to God, who is ever new and unique.

The life of God is unique; but it is also *eternal*. The many-colored little bit of life that he gives us on this earth looks like nothing by comparison. It is a life in time, hemmed in, inwardly threatened and disunited. Yet within it lies the grace of participating in eternal life: with the help of God's grace, our finite life opens onto his eternal life, and he pours his own life into ours. A man who does not believe in God will try to arrange his earthly life, his eighty years, cutting and measuring it out as one does a piece of cloth.

He will devote ten years to one occupation, ten years to another, dividing it in portions like a good housekeeper, and with "luck" he may perhaps carry out his plan. But plans of that kind end abruptly the moment a man knows in faith that life is in the Word and that earthly life opens out onto eternal life. Then there is no longer any point in planning, because one's whole life belongs to God. He no longer wants to arrange his life, because he is deprived of any standard of measurement. Each moment of his life is turned toward eternal life. The plan is in the hands of God, and his life is no longer limited. Eternal life comes alive in time, and earthly life in time becomes really worth living.

But there is also *death*. Death, too, is willed and created by God. Death is not evil and foreign to God: the limit of eternal life. On the contrary, God has power over death, just as, being eternal light, he has power over darkness. In the first place, death is a sign that the creature's life is inwardly limited and therefore belongs to God. Death is the seal of God's power over the life of his creature. Death is not merely the outward limit of life but permeates the whole course of earthly life. Without the ferment of death, finite life would not be life. The vitality of an organism is manifested in the constant dying and renewal of its cells, and, what is more, the dying cells are the younger and more vital, whereas the newly formed cells are "older" from the point of view of vitality. In order to remain alive, the organism perpetually has to die, and that is the life through which it proceeds to death. The process of spiritual development is the same: the ripeness and wisdom of age are not an apparent but a real phase of life and are always the result of a progressive limitation of the field of vision, involving the rejection of more and more possibilities. Resignation is part of the ripeness of age. There, too, life bears death within it. It is there that the creature displays his limitations and God shows him his power over life. And so it may seem as though the creature were like God insofar as living, and differed from God and were separated from him insofar as mortal. As though God showed us death and his power over death simply in order to focus our attention on eternal life, by means of the contrast.

But in another sense, both life and death are images of God. Of course, one cannot say that death, as an end, is in any sense in God, since his eternal life is unending. But if death is understood to mean the sacrifice of life, then the original image of that sacrifice is in God as the gift of life flowing between Father and Son in the Spirit. For the Father gives his whole life to the Son, the Son gives it back to the Father, and the Spirit is the outflowing gift of life.

This "living death" is the absolute opposite of the death of sin in which man ceases giving (the life for which he is made) and imprisons himself within the limits of his finite life. In doing so, he cuts himself off from eternal life and delivers himself up body and spirit to that death which consists in separation from eternal life. In this sense, death is both sin itself and the consequence of sin. And for a man like that, who is really dead, God's eternal life is deadly.

God's relation to death is transformed by the redemption. Before the birth of Christ, to see God was to die, because the sinner could not bear the abundance of love, of giving, of devotion and sacrifice in the eternal life of God; the sinner died, burned up and consumed. For sinful death and sacrificial death are as fire and water, opposites that have nothing in common. The death of sin is annihilated by the death of Christ on the Cross, and man's natural death is transformed, becoming a vessel fit to contain the eternal life of God. Age in mind and body receives an entirely new meaning. It no longer imprisons the creature in himself. In Christian life, there is no such thing as age, for every moment of earthly life opens onto eternal life. Every end becomes a new beginning. The aspect of God that spelled death to man is no longer a limit upon which he is broken to pieces, but the revelation of the living God that demands mortification, requiring that we die to our successive "limits" in order to receive new life from God. But this life is the devotion and surrender between Father and Son in the Holy Spirit. It may be that the intensity of God's life burns and consumes a man, but always in such a way as to form a transition, a breathing space, and as a preparation for a still higher life.

Christ overcame death in the world. Death has thus become different. In the night of the Cross, God himself, through the Son, experienced abandonment and surrender in the form of sinful death and experienced something that he did not know in eternal life. Thus he received human death into eternal life. In the loving surrender between Father and Son in the Holy Spirit lay the opening and the entrance into God through which earthly death was taken up into eternal life. The death of sin is annihilated, and the death that remains became a form and a vessel for the divine life. And in this way, death underwent a change—not only in its relation to us but also in its relation to the Trinity. It is no longer foreign to the Trinity. The Son tasted death during his estrangement from the Father, and through him the Father tasted death during his estrangement from the Son. Even the Holy Spirit, the source of life in God, is moved by their estrangement, for during the darkness of the Passion the source of life was, as it were, sealed off. It only begins to pour forth its gifts again when the Son returns to the Father. And so the marks of death (like the wounds in the Son's body) are visible in the Holy Spirit: he surrenders himself more completely, as it were, gives himself more perfectly; a possibility has been made manifest that could not even be suspected before the Passion.

The mysteries of this unlimited self-surrender and abandonment on the Cross, and of the night of darkened understanding, are further forms of God's supreme vitality, the fulfillment of the life of love. That is why the Lord could wipe out death and transform it into life by dying. In the world, death is a limitation, a conclusion, an end. In God, death is always the beginning of new life. When a man dies from the earthly point of view, he lives on in God as eternal life. With his death, with his disappearance from the visible world, a place becomes vacant, but it does not remain empty. God takes possession of it. From a worldly point of view, a man's death leaves a gap in the life of his friends and of those who loved him. But that gap makes room for God in men's hearts. It is a reminder of God and is a source of devotion and surrender to God; it is seized and filled by God. *De mortuis nil nisi bene*, we say. And, in fact, our picture of the dead is gradually transformed; in our thoughts, we attribute more and more good to him, more divine qualities; imperceptibly we idealize him, and under his gaze we try to live differently and better. The dead, in fact, really live in God, and through death God's life is revealed more clearly to us. Since Christ's death, all eternal life springs from death.

THE WORD AS LIGHT

1:4b. *And the life was the light of men.*

All created life strives. It is an impulse, an unrest, impossible to still or satisfy, always striving for something to satisfy and still it, in which to rest and bask. The sphere, the kingdom in which life finds rest is *light*. Plants, too, strive toward the light, unfold and bask in it. The creature's life strives toward the eternal life of God as to the light in which it comes to rest. For eternal life is the opposite of the dark impulses of finite life: it is all peace and clarity and thus the sphere in which the darkness of the world is appeased and clarified.

Before the death of Christ, eternal life was unapproachable and spelled death to the sinner; man could look upon the eternal light of God only from a distance. God only showed it to him; he never gave it to him. Man lived in an inadequate light. The light of eternal life was only given to us, really given to us as our own, in the Son. Until then, the light lay beyond our horizon: those who tried to approach it were burned and consumed and blinded. But the grace of Christ comes between God's light and our darkness to temper God's fire, to make it bearable for us and to act as an intermediary. We can see the Father in the Son without having to die.

Life and light are not absolutely the same. Life means giving and surrender; light is participation. Life unfolds, expands, and spreads; light takes possession of the space thus created. Life is tension; light is relaxed, redeemed. Life is individual, personal, unique; light is the link, the general, the universal. Life is faith; light is love. Life is what is; light is the radiation of being, its riches, its glory, its beauty. If there were no light, there would be no life, because life desires the light and wants to unfold as life in the light. Light, in contrast, is present everywhere, as a matter of course, making no demands. Not all beings have the same share of life, but all participate equally in the light.

In the Church, too, in the Body of Christ, one member possesses more life than another; some receive more grace than others and more eternal life. But insofar as the life is the light of men, all share equally in the light. They are all bathed in the same light. We want and ask the Lord for more of his life, but not for more of his light. We soon have enough light; it is more than we can bear. We always cry out for more life (whether we accept what is offered us, always far richer than we realize, or whether we do not), but we are shy of more light because it overwhelms us. If we love someone who is as intelligent as he is beautiful, we naturally want to share more and more of his knowledge. But his beauty, on the contrary, is indivisible; we always possess it in full without being able to ask for more, in spite of the fact that we experience it as an inexhaustible grace. Wisdom can be communicated gradually and piecemeal, but one can only radiate beauty; it is an atmosphere surrounding them, like charm, an open secret that no one can explain. Life and light in God are related in a similar way. We strive toward his life in faith, are bathed in his light, and unfold in his love.

God is also life and light in the Church. His life is revealed in the sacraments and in preaching, his light through the presence of the Church in the world. Even the visible Church building and the presence that fills it are God's light. But his light is strongest where prayer is selfless. The life of God in the Church is an event, an action, an effect, and man answers to it in action. The light of God in the Church is an impersonal radiation of light; it is the answer of God to man's contemplation.

The Mass is a drama, the tragedy of the Lord; his life, his suffering, his effect are alive in the Mass, and our personal lives and suffering and work are taken up into it. It is an event that moves from person to person, from life to life. The grace that it communicates is measured and proportioned to the individual believer: at Mass, each individual receives the strength to make his Christian life, his suffering, and his work more vital. It is not a matter of indifference to the vitality of the Mass whether the individual Christian takes part in it or not. Each individual Mass is an act of God that is more completely fulfilled and more filled with life if the congregation participates in the act. It is fulfilled in the congregation. It is a unique act, today's act, in which yesterday and tomorrow play no part.

Light, in contrast, is not an act at all, but a condition. It is not relative to the life of the individual, but absolute; it stands above his life. It is unaffected by the limitations of the congregation; it is the grace of God offered and poured out, regardless of whether it is gathered up or not—though of course one cannot remain remote from the life of the Church without harm to the light. The more prayers people say, the more life there is, the greater the light will be. But it remains true that in communicating life, God stoops to the individual, whereas in the communication of his light, he draws the individual into his light, allows him to sink and dissolve in that light. In prayer, man goes into the light in the same way that a number goes into a sum total that is complete without it and does not need to be rounded off.

This light, which ignores personal limits and has no form, is *contemplation*. It is both God's contemplation and ours. It is what he shows us of himself, but it is equally our power to see it through grace. It is also the divine that inundates us and deprives us of any standard we may still possess for measuring his life. Contemplation is the nourishment of our souls, just as beauty is the nourishment of our senses, but it is nourishment that is not consumed as we feed upon it, just as light does not diminish according to the number who look at it. When the life of God is accepted, it is altered, and God receives back something different from what he gave us. His light, in contrast, is unchangeable; it simply absorbs us.

Now there is no opposition between life and light in God, for the life we are told is the light of men. One cannot live without light, though one can only see and receive the light when one is already alive. The unbeliever who goes into a church will be quite insensible to the light of God that radiates from it. And a Christian who limits himself to the life, who is entirely absorbed in the active, liturgical, charitable life of the Church but who does not listen and attend passively to the voice and light of God will not be able to take part in the true and fruitful life of the Church. His reception of the sacraments becomes purely symbolic; their real power to fill him is held down. The life cannot unfold in him to the light and is therefore no true life. He fails to perceive the contradiction in desiring life without light. An inner blindness, a torpor prevents him seeing it. It is a dangerous form of death and sets in among the pious, without their noticing it, if they extend action farther and farther afield at the cost of contemplation and put their own good works in the place of the work of God.

But the relation between the two, between life and light, between action and contemplation, is wonderfully free in the Church; there is no universal rule to regulate their relationship. Every Christian must live in both and is free to shape this double life himself. No final equilibrium between the two realms can ever be established; the movement of life between the two, passing from one to the other, must never be allowed to die down.

God's life is *the light of men*, but it is also the life of men. God's life, in itself infinitely one, is given to us both as life and as light. Where we are concerned, it divides itself in two: into life and light. Otherwise, we could not grasp God's eternal unity and life. We should have no access to it, no point of contact, no foothold from which to grasp its formlessness. The unity of God is broken up for our sakes into facets and aspects, but we must always remember that these facets are only points of view and do not correspond to the sum of the reality of God. We cannot acquire the unity of God as though it were a total to be gathered together piecemeal. It is better to say that behind each aspect lies the whole inconceivable mystery of God's unity. When God reveals one aspect of his life to us, he creates more room in us, an opening for something greater. But even if we were entirely open, if there were nothing left in us to be expanded, we should still be completely shut in and imprisoned compared with him. His revelations are but indications—a point compared to a line, a plane surface compared to a concrete body. The whole creation is but a hint of what he is. In heaven this hint will be expanded: we shall see what his Kingdom is and ultimately what he is; but even that vision, though forever expanding, will never be complete. Nevertheless, there will be nothing humiliating in learning more and more about him, because his very being is the "evermore", and our apprehension of God will be a growing capacity to allow ourselves to be filled by the abundance of his light.

THE WORD IN THE DARKNESS

1:5. *The light shines in the darkness, and the darkness has not overcome it.*

God is light, and there is no darkness in him that his light cannot master. For darkness is certainly not unknown to him; he created day and night just as he created death with life. Darkness, too, belongs to God and falls under his authority. And so there are three kinds of night: the night created by God, the quality of God that led him to create night, and finally the night of sin created by man.

The darkness in God is only an aspect of his eternal light. His light is impenetrable and remains an eternal mystery. Its blinding light strikes us as darkness because we cannot endure it, and his greatest brilliance often seems to us to be darkness itself. When a man loses everything and despairs and is then told that God is love, the words throw him into a still darker night of despair. Although God himself is light and nothing else, and although there is no darkness in him, nevertheless his darkness does not consist solely in the fact that we fail before his light. It is better to say that night, which he created, is an image and similitude of one of the qualities of his unapproachable light.

In the world, God divided light from darkness, though he himself is above this distinction. Because God parted the two, we imagine we know what light and darkness are. In our world, they meet and merge one into the other, and we reckon with them as with two absolutes. We reckon with what appear to be their culminating points—with midday and midnight—and starting from there divide the rest of the day and the night accordingly. When we think of God as light, we imagine him to be that half of our time called by us day. And yet day and night are only a faint image of what God, as eternal light, possesses. In the beginning, God divided night from day and gave us the day in which to work and the night for rest. In himself he made no such distinction—he is beyond the world he made, in which everything is dispersed in contraries— but, being creatures, we try to separate one thing from another in thinking of him, in order to gain a foothold, a basis for our concepts. We long to survey God; we like to divide light from darkness in him, what we understand from what we do not understand. But it is not possible, and, where we are concerned, his light contains an element of darkness.

Suppose a man is at death's door, a man who has lived like most men, knowing he would die one day and familiar with the idea of judgment and responsibility—though death and God were very remote. Of God he merely knew that there were a few commandments that served to keep a certain degree of order in the world, certain rules in the game of good and evil, and a few regulations for one's religious behavior. A man like this suddenly finding himself face to face with death and knowing that he will shortly enter God's light will probably try to make a hurried reckoning of his life, a balance sheet of good and evil, a rough account of his virtues and sins. But the closer he looks at his life, the less clear the account appears; he can no longer distinguish light from darkness. A sense of dread invades him. He may try to escape it by clutching at the thought that he was no worse than others, that he was an average man, when suddenly he realizes that in a few minutes he will be standing before God where the average means nothing; a feeling of panic adds to his confusion, and he realizes that for all his distinctions he is only getting bogged down in his own darkness. In that state of mind, he gives up the attempt and turns to prayer, and his prayer is perhaps the first beginning of real faith in God, the first real surrender of his life to God. To him and to those like him, the light of God appeared in the darkness.

In the world, light and darkness are mutually exclusive: where the light penetrates, the darkness is dispersed and thrown open. For God separated light from darkness. But in God there are no contradictions. One can say that both are the expression of his goodness, of his essence, or that darkness is a characteristic of his light, or that light and darkness are both characteristics of the inconceivable light that passes understanding. The darkness of God is the aspect of his light we do not understand.

That is why darkness is God's preserve, the visible sign of his power and of his eternal authority. He reserves the darkness for himself and does not give it to us. He has planted a hedge around paradise, and the fact that he reserves the darkness for himself is one of the mysteries of his love. We ought to learn in faith and in love to respect this mystery, because it is perhaps the greatest mark of his love and will be revealed to us one day if he wishes. He wishes us, in fact, to come up against limits in our lives, and from that we should learn humility and self-surrender. But in our want of faith and love, of confidence and self-surrender, we always want to go beyond the limits set us in order to get beyond the mystery of darkness. We imagine that our being excluded from God's darkness is an arbitrary act on his part, forbidding us something, and we cannot bear being deprived of anything. We overlook the fact that darkness is necessary. The light needs it in order to flow on eternally, in order to have still more space to penetrate, conquer, and measure. In fact, God's light has the night within it, as a shell, a veil, a hiding place for the essential mystery, as a protection for its love. The mysterious character of love is what man cannot endure, and so he breaks bounds.

And finally, love needs the mystery that surrounds it because it is vulnerable and defenseless. That is why night becomes the zone of danger and temptation. The moment we commit the sin of not enduring the dark night of love, of wanting to throw light on the darkness of God, night becomes the symbol of sin. The sin consists in not enduring the mystery. Man wants to know what God does in the hours of darkness he has reserved to himself. That distrust is the contrary of faith and the death of love. For love implies and presupposes mutual faith, and it can live only as long as that confidence survives. We try to replace a loving faith by knowledge, and that prevents us believing the lover's secret can be the mystery of perfect love. Love must never seek to change into knowledge, for knowledge can never be the measure of love. Love certainly presupposes knowledge of what one loves, but the moment love begins, one no longer loves merely in proportion to one's knowledge, for, after all, one loves more than the characteristics of the person one loves; one loves him himself, whose essence and kernel are always beyond one's knowledge. But because man did not accept the limited knowledge given to him by God, because he wanted to compare his light with the light of God, he fell into the night of sin.

The darkness of sin is the antithesis of the darkness of God, and it sets God's light in the contrary light, the light of a loveless knowledge. The darkness of sin has two aspects, an objective and a subjective. Objectively, the sinner's persistence in darkness consists in his falling away from the light and the life of God, in falling from grace, and thus in spiritual blindness. This blindness is both an inability to see and a refusal to see. Not being able to see is the objective; not wanting to see is the subjective aspect of darkness. In the second instance, the sinner draws back into the darkness and entrenches himself there. True love is always naked before the beloved, even if it does not avow everything and preserves its secret.

But with people one does not love, one wraps oneself up in a sort of artificial darkness. One intentionally displays one aspect or another of one's self; one clothes oneself in armor. This armor is, of course, useless against the light of God, for his light penetrates our artificial darkness all the same. But we ourselves fly from his light and love our own darkness more than the light.

Yet even when we are entirely lost in our sins and there is no way out of our darkness back into the light of God, our darkness and his light are not absolute contraries. The darkness of sin is not beyond the power of God. That is why it is possible for God in his grace to envelop our sinful darkness in his greater darkness and to conceal from us our own unbearable darkness, for the sinner is so wretched that unless God concealed his misery from him, he would die.

The light of God now *shines in the darkness* of sin. It not only shines as far as the darkness; it shines into the darkness. The moment in which the light enters the darkness is the moment of the Passion. While the Lord hangs on the Cross and his whole being overflows upon the world—body, soul, divinity, and love—and everything that he has assumed and received from us—hate, tepidity, insufficiency—overflows in love for the sins of the world: that is the moment when the light penetrates the darkness. That is the center point from which the light is diffused throughout the whole world. That is why everything must be seen as from the Cross.

The *love of the Lord* on the Cross, surrendering itself to the darkness, is threefold. It is, in the first place, the love that assumed the sacrifice, that consented to surrender itself. Secondly, it is love in the act of being surrendered, love in the consummation of the sacrifice. And finally, it is love after the consummation of the sacrifice: in emptiness and death, love already surrendered. Although the three states of love fuse into each other on the Cross, they are the three states that mark and articulate Christ's earthly life: the Incarnation is the Son's consent to the sacrifice to which the Father sends him; his life on earth is the consummation of the sacrifice; his death on the Cross and descent into hell are the state of the consummated sacrifice, of the victim and host.

At the foot of the Cross is the *Mother of the Lord*, who participates in the sacrifice. Though in her case, the sequence is lived in the reverse order. She gives her consent at the foot of the Cross; the birth of the child in Bethlehem is the consummation of the sacrifice; and when the child was conceived in Nazareth, she was already the victim, given to God. This reversal of the order reveals her very being as woman: her end is already in her beginning. Her whole destiny as a mother is sealed and consummated in conceiving: she lives *from* the Cross, while Christ, being man, lives in the opposite direction, *toward* the Cross.

The Lord's suffering on the Cross is embodied and expressed in the threefold wounds: the wounds in his head caused by the crown of thorns; the wounds in his hands and feet caused by the nails; the wound in his heart caused by the lance. The head wounds go least deep, but spiritually they are the most painful, suffered for man's scorn of the spirit, for the sceptic, the cynic, the denials. The wounds of the nails are those that ridicule the Father in the Son and expiate the sins of the flesh—in the widest, most all-embracing sense of the word—wherever the creative work of the Father is misused. The wound in the side is in expiation of the sins against the Son and his divine-human love. These threefold wounds, which are in themselves darkness, transform the darkness of sin and redeem it into light. The redemption, again, has three aspects: first of all, it is the affirmation of Spirit, through which the sins of the sceptic and the cynic are expiated. Secondly, there is the bodily suffering of the Passion, which expiates the sins of the flesh. And finally, in the state of utter emptiness of heart in death, Christ redeems the sinners who are only converted, changed, and brought back by the Lord after death, on the threshold of hell, in sight of hell.

The light that pours out from the Cross strikes upon the darkness, which does not receive it. This darkness is sin, and sin is the *hatred* of the world for love. Hatred has three forms. In the first place, love is rejected because hatred hates, because it will not allow itself to be moved and roused; spiritually, it is preoccupied with itself and does not want to love. Secondly, because hatred simply does not see the light and for that reason does not recognize itself as hate and would be amazed to be told that it hated, for it regards itself as love, just as it takes what is really death and darkness for life and light. Thirdly, love is rejected because hatred offers no surface upon which it can "take", because hatred is turned away from God in such a way that nothing in it can be illuminated by the light of God. As such, this third form of hate is amorphous, no longer a finite, earthly hate, but a hate from the world below. These three forms of hate are the negatives corresponding to the three wounds of the redemption. And the light of love is poured from the

Cross into these three forms of darkness, the light that is given, sacrificed, and poured out.

But light and darkness have not always been related in the same way. Behind the Cross, in the distance, is the *Old Covenant*. In it, too, was the light of revelation, which came into the world in three stages: as the coming grace, which sought out man; as grace received, which redeems him; and as effective grace, which works in man. But the Son was not yet revealed in the Old Covenant; the shaft of light was not separated from the Father; and grace remained, as it were, hovering above the world; the redemption was in suspension. The coming of grace, its reception, and its effect occurred only in a sort of symbolic manner, the real meaning of which was still hidden; indeed, its coming was at the same time withholding, its acceptance a rejection, its effect without result. Light and darkness were not really separated or—which amounts to the same thing—not really soaked one in the other. For substitution was as yet unknown; because love was everywhere constrained and held back. Darkness was still a reserved sphere and could not be touched; it had not been freed by the Father so that it could be pierced through and through by the light.

Nearer the Cross is the period of the Lord's public life before the Passion, the period of the Sermon on the Mount. That is where most of the Synoptic teaching belongs, where the light appears in the darkness and shines into hatred. But it does not shine as it will shine from the Cross. Here again, the light is threefold. First of all, it shines in such a way that hatred does not comprehend it or receive it, knowing too well what love implies and what the consequences of acceptance would be. Hatred is afraid of the consequences and will not take them upon itself; that is why it hates. Secondly, the light strikes upon hate that takes itself for love but does not see the real consequences of love. Its way of receiving the light is pharisaical. Thirdly, the light meets hate in the form of the tepid, those who no longer have the strength to make a decision, who cannot say Yes or No, having lost the capacity to receive the light. This form of hatred is blind because there is not a single spot on its surface that is sensitive to light and darkness, and one cannot force light or color upon it. It is what God has spewed out.

Jesus' relation to this last form of hate—which is the eternal hate of the beyond—is different at the period of the Sermon on the Mount and on the Cross. The Father leaves the Son free to do as he wills. The Son has authority by virtue of his mission and as the Father's representative. But God had already rejected this form of hate, and that cannot be undone. The Son must therefore fulfill his mission within the sphere allotted to him: the outer darkness already rejected by God lies beyond his authority. That is the stage of the New Covenant before the Passion and of the Cross before the real redemption. It is also the watershed between the Old and the New Covenants. From this it may be clearly seen that the New Covenant itself is a movement, a dramatic event in which the light enters the darkness, gradually forcing its way into the darkness of death. This happens in the Passion, particularly in the third and mysterious form of suffering, in which, after the consummation of the sacrifice, the Lord becomes the offered victim, the host.

The movement of the New Testament is *the movement of Christ* himself: as the Word, he remains with the Father in the beginning and nevertheless goes out from the Father and returns to him through the darkness. Christ is first of all the Son, secondly the representative sent by the Father, and thirdly the one who returns to the Father. As the Son, he does the will of his Father. As his representative, he is given authority and acts upon his own judgment. As the one returning, he administers the mandate of mankind before the Father. As the Son, his work consists in helping men to salvation from their sins within their earthly lives. As the Father's representative, he effects the salvation of mankind taken as a whole and in the beyond after death. As the one returning to the Father, he effects the total eternal movement from sin to grace, and this for every individual life, for each and every man. In this third state and action, he is the host or victim given to each, and this in his return to the Father, which begins on the Cross. As Son, he works through the Word of God and speaks only of God, and he never appears so little as the Son as when thus speaking, for he was not speaking of himself but of the Father. Speaking as the Father's representative, he speaks in the first person: I am come; I am the light; I am the Son. Returning to the Father, he speaks of committing his spirit into his Father's hands—and the emphasis in the words on the Cross falls on "the hands of the Father", not upon "my spirit". His surrender is complete, because from now on he is in fact visibly and undeniably the host and victim, the real presence, and needs to speak only of God. This state begins after his death on the Cross, not only after the Ascension. Christ once again acts as Son. He returns to his first state, having performed the work he was sent to do as the Father's representative. But he returns as Spirit to that work and as such works immediately in each and every man.

The words of love with which Christ gives himself back to the Father in death: "Father, into your hands I commit my spirit"—the words, that is, that link the first verse— "*The Word was with God*"—to the fifth verse—*The light shines in the darkness*—these words themselves have three depths of meaning. In them, Father and Son are related in a threefold manner to each other. They mean, in the first place: Father, I give you back my spirit; in your hands it is safe, for you are my Father. In the second place, they mean: Father, I give you my spirit although I no longer know you, no longer know whether you exist or not, since you have become full of darkness. Thirdly and finally, they mean: I commit my spirit into your hands, which are not hands but spirit; and if they are spirit, then I am born of your spirit. For since you bore me as Son, Father, you gave yourself to me; you no longer possessed yourself, but I possessed you and, as your representative, revealed you to the world. But now my mission is fulfilled, it is consummated; now I no longer possess you, but you hold me once again in your hands, which are spirit. I no longer bear you, but you bear me. I give you back the spirit I received from you. I give you back the Kingdom, that you may be all in all.

Through all this, the trinitarian meaning of the Cross shines more and more strongly, the meaning of the Cross as the light that shines in the darkness. For the final darkness in which the crucified light of love shines is not the darkness of the world's hate, but the darkness of God during the separation of Father and Son in which the Holy Spirit participates. Each threefold division that refers to the Son in his suffering is a closer or more distant reflection of the Trinity during the Passion. During the Passion, Father and Son are mutually and reciprocally light and darkness. The darkness of the Son's abandonment has its origin in the Father's darkness. Darkness is the Father's preserve, the sphere that as Creator he divided from the light and over which he reserves authority: night and sin. His authority over this sphere is the rightful judgment he will hold. And the Son assumes this darkness on the Cross, for he is the perfect image of his Father, then and always, and the Father recognizes his own darkness once again in the crucified Son. That is the fellowship of Father and Son in its final form, in the form of final separation.

From eternity the relation between Father and Son was the relationship of life and love, and on earth the Son continued to live on his relation with the Father. The contact of which he had always been sensible is now broken. The fellowship between them is expunged. They become strangers to each other; their light and their darkness no longer correspond. The Father's darkness is no longer the safe mystery of love, into which the Son's light can penetrate. It is something foreign, cold, hostile, and unknown, which repels. And by this very fact, the Father's darkness becomes light. For now that he sees darkness in the Son in his state of abandonment, he no longer demands it as his own. He can regard sin in the creature in the light of his Son's love instead of in the darkness of justice. Thus the Father's darkness becomes light in the Son as well as in the Father. And in the opposite sense, the Father's darkness, too, proceeds from that of the Son, from his will to suffer and his obedience in suffering. The Father suffers not only through having to allow the Son to suffer but also because the Son suffers of his own free will. He so loved the Son that he allowed it and really suffered because the Son entered and embraced suffering. At the end of the Passion, the Father's excessive love becomes light for the Son; in this light he gives back his darkness; and the Father's love also becomes power, the power that awakens him out of the darkness of death.

The period of the mutual abandonment of Father and Son is the period in which the most secret mystery of their love is fulfilled. Their estrangement is a form of their supreme intimacy. Now if the Holy Spirit is the living exchange of love between Father and Son, he too is touched by the darkness between them. In their state of abandonment, he is, as it were, obliterated; he becomes invisible and transparent; he leaves the Father and the Son alone in their supreme intimacy. He extinguishes himself—and in that sense becomes darkness—so that nothing remains but the mystery of the darkened love of Father and Son. Being the love between them, the Holy Spirit is also the darkening of their love. That is the form in which he participated in the crucifixion and in the redemption. His darkness assumes the form of absence. But for that very reason, he is more present than ever and yields up his final mystery in the Passion. On Calvary he became so transparent as to be invisible, so that when the Holy Spirit shines forth at Easter, he is transparent light and is poured forth in limpid water. Thus he leaves the Father and the Son alone in their suffering as though standing aside and then takes over the role of witness. He is the Third Person, to whom both have given their hand in suffering. His testimony makes God's decision irrevocable. And though the Spirit lays aside the role of witness the moment Father and Son are reunited, when he once again becomes their common life, it is nevertheless the Holy Spirit we can call to witness and invoke whenever we are tempted to doubt the reality of that incredible and inconceivable night. He was present during the tragedy, and it was he, in God, who bore the suffering, and, on the Son's return, he becomes the bearer of joy.

And finally, the light shining in the darkness of the Cross is the birth of a new mankind, the *Church*. The Church springs from the mystery of the Cross in which darkness ceases to be the preserve of the Father and is penetrated through and through by the light of love.

Human society itself, fundamentally that between man and woman, has the form of light and darkness. Each sees and feels in the other its natural antithesis, the unfamiliar and (behind the light of a superficial understanding) darkness. In sin, this natural antithesis deepens into a tragic opposition, so that the sexual relationship (insofar as it is not open to the grace of the Cross) and all sensual love becomes darkness instead of an expression of Christian love. But through Christ, sensual love receives the innocence of grace; the reciprocal darkness and solitude of man and woman give birth to the light of the child in whose God-given and grace-bearing being the love of the parents is sealed and spiritualized. The explosion of this egoism *à deux*, the image and effect of which is the child, but whose origin is ultimately God, occurs in every form of society.

In all I and Thou relationships, love is both life and light. As life, it is the bestowal of personal affection; as light, it is a universal love radiating in all directions: the love of God and of one's neighbor. If love is not light, its life suffocates. It is not only in the family but also in the wider circle of society as a whole that the light begins shining in the darkness. Love must allow others to be other; it must accept the proximity of other circles, in which others are related, not to it, primarily, but to God. It is only by letting others alone and leaving things to God that one learns that the neighbor one does not know belongs to God, and then the light of real helpfulness and true community becomes possible. It is only when we set our neighbor free, when we recognize and respect his darkness because it is open to the mystery of God, that our reciprocal strangeness is endurable and is even transformed into the light of a, as it were, contemplative view of our neighbor in God.

All this is fulfilled in the relation between Christ and the Church, the relationship that gives its final and redeemed form to the relation of man and woman and to every form of human society. For the relation between Christ and the

Church, too, is the relation of light to darkness. In the first place, Christ is light, and the Church is darkness; it is even the darkness proper in which the light of the Cross shines redeemingly. But since the light of the Cross burns itself out to the absolute end, and the whole effect of its light is transposed into the Church, the Church is light and Christ is darkness. For Christ's love became weakness, while the Church is the power and the glory of Christ. The community of the Church is born of their reciprocal darkness; it is their child and as such is light, and (though always concealed from them) the Holy Spirit lives in the community.

The Church sprang from the Cross at the moment when the Son returned to the Father to become the Word in the beginning. It lives from the Word that was with God in the beginning, that is with God and is God. This Word, which was with him in its going forth and in its return, is the Word of the Church and is with God in three ways for the Church: it is promise, grace, and judgment. It is promise insofar as the Church is the ever expected. It is grace for the Church that is always arising. It is the judgment of the Word upon the Church that is always failing and falling, a judgment that leads the Church back again to unity with God. To that unity with God which is not indeed destroyed in the true community but which does not always adhere to all the members and limbs of the hierarchy of the Church. This Church, with her failures and imperfections, returns through the judgment to grace, to take up the promise ever and again. After realizing the threat of the Word's judgment, she is granted a time of grace because she cannot as yet bear the fulfillment of the promise; hers is the happiness of always finding her way back from the unfaithfulness of the whore to the faithfulness of the Bride, before taking up once again, and herself assuming, the promise. With Christ the man, the movement is a forward one; with the Church, the woman, the movement is a return. The fact that the Word was in the beginning with God means, too, that, where the Church is concerned, it is also the end.

THE WORD AS FAITH, LOVE, HOPE, AND MISSION

1:6–8. *There was a man sent from God, whose name was John. He came for testimony, to bear witness to the light, that all might believe through him. He was not the light, but came to bear witness to the light.*

Up to this point, the subject of the Prologue has been the Word that was with God. The world was considered in the Word, insofar as it is with God and is God. But now the viewpoint changes, for a man came into the world pointing to God from the world, to God, and to the light of the Word.

The content of the Baptist's existence is to direct attention away from himself, the world, and to point toward the true light, which he is not and which is in God. The beginning and origin of his action is a mission: he is *sent from God*; the essence of his action is faith, and as true faith it includes love and hope. The fact that there could be a mission consisting in pointing toward the light, in a testimony and in faith presupposes that the Word—the Word that is with God, that is life and light and shines in the darkness—itself came into the world. Came into the world, moreover, in such a way that its movement from the Father and back to the Father embraced the world; in such a way that, in being communicated to the world, the Word became the Word of grace, which the world could receive in faith, love, and hope.

Before the Word came in the flesh, there was a sense
of expectation and of insufficiency in the world. There
was an awareness of *emptiness*, of a void, though how
the void was to be filled was not known. The world expected some form of confirmation, of ratification, but
what came was utterly different from what was expected.
The world was in a stage prior to hope and prior to faith.
It could not believe in the possibility of faith. It dared not
hope to find hope on its path. It resembled those women
who always recognize the signs of pregnancy in others
but are never willing to believe in the promise of their
own motherhood. Or children going to school for the first
time: everything is different, strange, unfamiliar; life takes
a step forward that they cannot quite follow; they are full
of expectation, but expect the unknown, the unfamiliar.
Thus the world was full of an expectation that was neither
faith nor hope. This expectation, though awakened by the
Word, was not yet the real answer of grace. In its sense of
advent, the Old Covenant inclines toward the New, and
in the twilight appeared the man who was to bear witness
to the light.

The Word that was coming to fill the void of the
world's expectation was to prove itself not only a spoken
word but also an active, creative word. In its desire to
become the *grace* that fulfills the expectation of the world,
the Word simultaneously reaffirms the truth of the Creator's judgment, which had been rendered vain by sin:
"God saw that it was good." Christ has the redemption
of the world at heart, one might say, in order to offer the
Father a world that is good. His life in the world is so rich
in love and accepted grace that the affront and offense
done to the Father is abundantly repaid.

Before the coming of grace, all good was on the side
of God, and all evil on our side. But the Lord poured out

his grace, poured so much love into us, that the love in us outweighs the offense. All God's reckonings were upset: whereas formerly we were his debtors, a debt was now opened on God's side. But ultimately debts and accounts have no meaning where grace is concerned; the Son's return to the Father effaces this new debt again, and both are wiped out in the exchange of love—the one ultimately valid thing. In this love, man acknowledges his eternal debt to God, and God acknowledges his debt to us, for, enriched by the Son's sacrifice, the earth has loved God more than it has offended him. This love is not only meant externally for the world but is also poured into it; grace gives man an inward purity of his own that not only balances but also outweighs his sin.

The communication of the Word as grace means the communication of the Spirit of Christ, of the *Holy Spirit*, to the world. The Holy Spirit is poured forth from the Cross, in God, in the Church and the sacraments, and in the hearts of believers: he is the invisible, ever-present fluid that permeates and binds everything together. He is the communication and the gift of God as well as that in us which receives the gift of God. In him we are open to God, acknowledge God, and confess to God; he is the object that God gives us as well as the subject within our subject that receives him. He attains the height of explosive intensity when he vanishes from our sight on the Cross, and it is similarly as the invisible Mediator between God and man that he communicates the highest experience of union in love. Through this invisible presence of his, both between Father and Son and between God and the world, the Spirit is the true life, and it is he who gives form to love. If, for example, our daily Communion were only the meeting ground of Christ and sinner, if they alone met face to face, so inconceivable a dialogue would, in the long run, become monotonous and illusory. But the Spirit opens up new prospects daily and reveals new possibilities to us. He is variety itself, imagination, the very inexhaustibleness of love. And that is why he cannot abide habit and custom, an unalterable framework. He is forever opening up and stirring up the soul; he is the beginning and eternal youth.

The Word of God that is communicated to us in the Spirit and through the Spirit—the Word that was in the beginning, which is the light and the life of men and to which John testified—is *faith, love, hope.*

Faith, then, was in the beginning, and since there was nothing in the beginning but God, faith was in God. Until the creation, until there were men, faith was in God. And because the creature's word is deposited in God and, in going forth from God, is always in its origin with God, faith too is deposited in God. Faith is the creature's very foundation and comes before everything; God gives the creature this faith in creating him, not as an additional characteristic, but as an essential part of him. In the beginning, it is the creature's foundation; only subsequently does it become a characteristic, capable of being developed and qualified this way or that. In the first instance, there is nothing upon which it can grow or be shattered; it is absolute. There is nothing at first with which it can be compared—since there is no such thing as disbelief. It is only when love and hope are joined to faith that it can grow and increase and the comparative enters in.

Everything is created through faith; it is the life and the light of man. It shines in the darkness. Darkness is added as the second to the first, to the prime thing. Darkness enters faith only with the awakening of longing, when man becomes conscious that, as creature, he is separated from God and that God has placed him outside himself. In the beginning he was in God, but now he finds himself alone before God. In that instant, God gives man the second gift, withheld until then: *love*. The moment loneliness and the solitude of being outside God are felt, and there is the danger that man might try to stand on his own, independently of God, when the abyss of darkness yawns, and it is possible he may stumble and fall over his own I—in that same instant, God bridges the abyss with the gift of love and illuminates the darkness with the light of love—the love of God and of one's neighbor.

Love, however, is always knowledge. Yet as soon as it is born, it only has one aim, to overflow knowledge. Knowledge is always speculative; it is the conclusion of an operation, a sum total reached, a product, the result of a reckoning. Touching a person we do not yet know, we may say: I could perhaps love him; I shall perhaps love him; he might respond to me. And in doing so, one starts out from oneself; one takes stock of the position and estimates its advantages. Human love always begins with a sort of reckoning, with certain expectations. That is its nature, and it is neither selfish nor evil. But once love itself awakens, all the preliminaries are forgotten. Once love is set free, it can no longer be explained by its original demands. One no longer looks back at the original motives, and out of shame one does not even want to recall them. In the interval, love has become an elemental power. Love is always fullness, and fullness fills a want, but once the want has been filled, we no longer need to know that there was something to be filled. In its fullness, love is once again in God; it returns to the pure faith of its origin, which is fulfilled by pure love and thus learns to see.

But the path of love leads through one's neighbor. Love is not something abstract, but that close, enfolding, human movement that is the one victorious, progressive, and creative thing in life. It is also the one fruitful and warming thing. It begins to broaden out at its first contact with its neighbor and is not to be halted in its course until it reaches God. Anyone who loves his neighbor as himself, through the strength of God, can also love God himself. But there is no God where there is no Thou.

I cannot see God, so he has given me my brother as his image. He has thrown me out into the creation armed with absolute faith; but because absolute faith is deposited in God and remains with him, that absolute faith is at the same time taken from one, for only God is absolute, and I myself am relative. The absolute, the unconditional, comes back to me only in love. But as absolute faith is taken from me, I am given knowledge. God placed me in the world in a state of spiritual nakedness, with the task of living in the world. Up to now I only knew God in faith. I was not lonely because I was in God. But now I am outside God, and he leaves me to find the way back to him. It is here that knowledge awakens. The beginning of knowledge is need. In my need I seek and find Thou, so as to discover and learn in Thou all that I cannot learn about the divine in myself. Here lies another danger point. For knowledge of my neighbor may become the medium and mirror of self-knowledge and self-love. God has therefore made the Thou in his own image; everything in it is an image and symbol of what I know absolutely of God in faith. And that is why my longing for God must pass through my neighbor, who is an image of God.

I am outside, then, and have to find the way back to God. I do not as yet know myself (for sin has not awakened); I know myself only as I know a negative, and I seek God. I feel that I can no longer fly, without realizing that I can walk step by step along the road. As I begin to move along this path in the blindness of my first faith, the only measure of my distance from God is Thou; my neighbor is the means of my knowing my remoteness and my path. The Thou becomes my boundary and limit.

It comes naturally to me with my origin in God to move as in a boundless sphere, and unless I were brought up against a limit, I should pass by and through my neighbor as in a dream. My movements are those of a blind man who has heard a voice and goes toward it, unaccustomed to judging distances. For until now I had only known the voice of God and not as yet the limit of the Thou. Now I get to know that limit, and it is on that frontier that everything is decided. For it is there that faith becomes knowledge and there that knowledge can be surpassed through love. Love, at first latent and enveloped in longing, receives its true form in the experience gained on that frontier. In my blind longing, I expect the Thou to be great, good, and boundless, because God is so. But in Thou I come up against the finite; and of its limitation is born disappointment. This is salutary because love, until now a longing to fulfill one's own need, becomes longing for the fulfillment of the limited Thou. First of all, the I is placed outside God, deprived of the one thing necessary; and it has to look for the necessary where it is to be found: in its neighbor. But because the Thou appears limited and in need, the seeker, still in ignorance and wanting in knowledge, passes it by until he learns to permeate it with a growing insight and love. The fulfillment of the Thou grows with the growing knowledge of God. I try to give you to God so that you should learn to correspond better to God, so that the gap in you as between what you are and your original image in God should be closed, and in doing all this I love both God and you inseparably. My own incapacity no longer bothers me, because I now know that this incapacity of mine will only be made good in and through God. The love of God led me to my neighbor so that I should find God in him. The love of my neighbor leads me to God again because my neighbor can fulfill himself only in God, but also because my love for him can be fulfilled only in God.

The moment longing is transformed into the love of God and one's neighbor, love is in the beginning with God and is God, and everything is created through love and nothing is created outside love, and it is the light and the life of man. For God created man out of love and into love, and through love and for love. But having discovered sin, man could not bear life in love; he could not open his heart unconditionally to love and could not see that love is wholly to be found in love of his neighbor; and he did not give himself back to God. All that was said about the path of love remained an unfulfilled demand, which God could not fulfill because man would not love. And this because he longed for knowledge so intensely and became so intoxicated with it that he grew dissatisfied with the measure of knowledge given him by God. For the measure of knowledge that God allots man lies entirely within love; it is a factor within love, but being limited and adapted to man's estate, it was possible for man to pursue an aim beyond it. The tension between the sum of knowledge allotted to him and what man with this knowledge could think out for himself—using his speculative powers, the whole field open to his intelligence, the whole orbit of thought—this tension tempted him to overstep the measure God intended for him. That was sin. Man presumed and, using his knowledge, usurped what appertains to God and not to the creature: to be with God in the beginning, to be in the absolute, to be like God. Inebriated with his knowledge, he desired to drink the sea of the infinite.

God therefore gives man *hope* as the third. He gives him hope to help him endure not being God. To exist in a state of dependence. In doing so, he not only promises to take him back into himself but also gives him the proof of his constancy, by showing him the possibility of its fulfillment of his neighbor. By giving man his neighbor as the way, God gives him a pledge of his love and, in doing so, gives him hope. Man does not see God and only knows that he comes from God and has a presentiment of having been in God; he therefore needed an image of God that he could understand, so as to be able to hope in God and in the promise of his return to God. Knowing that my need is God, I can see that your need is God. The hope that I find in God really is the hope that God will become true to you. So that you should find him, God gives me hope as the path to you, and so to him. Hope, then, is the fulfillment of faith and love, assuming the reality of sin. The abyss that separates man from God is darker than the night and nothingness of creation, and that abyss, the abyss of sin, is bridged by hope.

Hope as such is the third. It is never the first; it is the completion of faith and love. It can never replace them. It must never be separated from them, or it becomes sin. True hope bears the form of faith and love: it must strive away from me toward my neighbor and God. God gives me real hope only when he has taken it from me to give it to you. Like faith and love, it remains deposited in God and enveloped in its beginning. All three are more in God than in us. In all three, we want to be more in God than in ourselves. In them our answer is enveloped in the original Word that was in the beginning with God. As a result of that envelopment, they are the life and the light of men.

To be a Christian means, therefore, to love one's neighbor and God in faith and, in doing so, to receive the gift of hope. It means to be so drawn to God and one's neighbor in all three (which are one) that we get to know absolutely nothing about ourselves, not even the sacrifice and the surrender involved. As long as the sacrifice of myself seems to me important, I am still imprisoned in my self, in my personal I. If a man were bitten by a snake, and a friend could save him only by sucking the poison out of the wound and dying of it himself—would he really think of himself and not simply of saving the man? Even if such a consideration arose of its own accord, he would reject the thought as utterly extraneous and, above all, as something to be concealed. The all-important thing is that I should not be a hindrance between you and God and that you should know that you owe life to God alone. But the man who is saved will not forget the one who saved him before God: he will see the sacrifice that overlooked itself, and he will not offend against neighborly love out of love for God—and thereby against the love of God itself that his savior had given him.

The self-forgetfulness of the Christian life never takes the form of a pious withdrawal from the world toward God. For the Word that was in the beginning with God and that came to us as faith, love, and hope came as the Word *sent* by the Father. Its going forth from God and its return to God spring singly and solely from its *mission*, its being *sent*. Even in God himself, the Word was sent out from all eternity from the Father in the Spirit, to return eternally in the love of the Spirit to the Father.

The existence of the Son is this: to portray the Father and so to reveal him. His existence is his mission. He came into the world as the Son who reveals the Father, being given the mission to show the Father to the world and, in his return, to lay the Kingdom (of faith, of love, and of hope), his Kingdom, at the feet of the Father. During his earthly mission, the Son conceals his own light, which he has deposited with the Father, so that, parting from his divinity, he may be nothing but the perfect messenger, merged and dissolved in his mission. He reveals his own light to the world by concealing it in the Father. It is the light of sonship, the light of his particular filial love as it shines toward the Father and toward man. In his mission, he has the power to deposit his light with the Father. The fact that man can and should do likewise derives from the fact that the Son does so. By nature, all men want their light to shine, and they try to show off their personalities. Any other course seems to them senseless. It is only when a man contemplates the Son's example that he understands that in imitating the Son he, too, must deposit his light with the Father.

It is precisely by concealing his light in the Father that the Son reveals not only the Father but himself to the world. For in doing so, he shows his love for the Father, which is so great that he renounces his own light.

His light is visible to man in faith, but as the light deposited in the Father. For the only way he can approach men is by shedding his divinity; then they can put their trust in him; then men can acknowledge his earthly appearance and include therein an affirmation of his divinity. In faith, he allows his hidden light to shine through the veil of its appearance and, as on Mount Tabor, to become visible. It is only after the Passion, in his return to the Father, that he clothes himself again in the light deposited in the Father; and it is only then that seeing and believing become one.

The Word, which is alive in us as loving, hoping faith, has for its form a mission, and consequently every Christian life in faith, love, and hope has the same form. This life is therefore not only an answer to the Father's Word, which enters and penetrates the world and returns to him out of the world. It is man's word, imitating and following the Word of God as it comes from God and returns to him. Man is not only a witness to the Word in the sense that he states what he sees, like an indifferent spectator or a lifeless wall reflecting the light that falls on it. In faith, love, and hope, we are given a living mission: namely, to bear witness to the light by means of the light of our faith, love, and hope. Just as the Son (who is the revelation of the Father) reveals himself in revealing the Father, so too the Christian witness testifies to his own mission in bearing witness to Christ. He does not testify to it in the same manner that Christ testifies to his coequal divinity, but he is given the power to point away from himself and testify to the light of the Word. In testifying that he is not himself the light, he testifies at the same time to the greatness of the grace that makes it possible for the light of God to be made visible through the darkness of man. He is not the light but a messenger, and, as one sent on a mission, he participates in the grace of the light. The movement with which he points toward the light is imparted to him by God; it is a shining movement of light to which God can add the grace of being a revelation of the light. Through grace, men can show one another God, give one another God, and reveal God to one another.

The mission of those who receive the Word of God in faith, love, and hope may have one of two forms. There are those (and they are the majority) whose mission is fulfilled within their faith, love, and hope. As believers, having faith, they are messengers of the light of their faith deposited in God, and God has sent them into the world in order that they should return to him through the world as men having confidence in God and seeking God. As men of love, their mission is not only to discover

God in their neighbor but also to show God and give God to their neighbor in his emptiness, need, and blindness. As men of hope, they participate in the mission of the Son, which includes their own, the fulfillment of which is given to them in the certainty of faith and in the confidence of love.

But apart from these, there is the little company of those who are marked out by God to give a special, qualified testimony. Their mission is not exhausted when they have fulfilled the demand, when their lives correspond to their life deposited in God, when they have radiated the grace they have received and understood returning to God as beginning anew in this world. That mission is universal and is realized to some extent in every Christian life. The witness singled out by God, on the contrary, receives a distinct and personal task directly from God. Part of this mission consists, in fact, in leading the life of an exceptional witness. That means placing one's whole personal life at the service of one's existence as a witness. The witness binds himself before God to sacrifice himself whole and entire to his mission. He binds himself to do so even before hearing what his mission is. Nor will he ever get to know the content of his mission fully and completely. He will have to listen and attend to it afresh every day. The content may change suddenly from top to bottom; it may change direction at any moment and may even turn into its contrary. While carrying out his mission, its real content will be concealed from the exception, and it will certainly not be something he can view as a whole. He must always be ready for everything. There is no resting in such a mission, for it springs directly from the very source of God's life.

The normal mission is something given with grace and though harmed by sin may be renewed through grace. But anyone failing in an exceptional mission is not entrusted with it again. His vessel is not only battered but also smashed to smithereens. He can indeed save himself personally, through the grace of God; but he is not given his mission a second time. The ordinary Christian mission may be interrupted; it can be set down like a burden, while one gets one's breath. An exceptional mission demands not only the whole of a man but also his whole time and every moment of his life. Those who fail in their ordinary mission do so, as a rule, out of weakness, through being lukewarm; but in the case of a qualified mission, the danger lies in underestimating it, in taking things easy and basking in its light instead of living solely for an eternal task. Failure means that great pride is never far distant, because the source of an exceptional mission rises in the immediate neighborhood of God. It calls for great self-assurance, only it must be an assurance rooted in God, and it does not tolerate the slightest admixture of pride.

This type of mission is indeed given to individuals, but primarily it concerns the Church. The Church as a whole has to live the life of the witness singled out by God, that is to say, in uninterrupted, lasting, and exclusive readiness to hear and carry out the ever-new message of God. The ever-new message is always opaque and formless, and neither Church nor individual understands it fully; it can therefore never be set aside and dismissed as though it were something already known. God's new injunctions cannot be discharged by pointing to already existing institutions. Very often God's new demands require the creation of a new framework, even if there are more than enough old ones to hand. Each and every Christian participates in the explicit testimony of the Church, but the distinction between the ordinary and the exceptional witness never corresponds simply to laity and priests.

The first exceptional witness to the light of Christ was *John the Baptist*. He is the criterion and image of every subsequent form of testimony and mission. That is why his place in the Prologue is such an important one: he appears clad with his mission even before the Word appears in the flesh. He is the witness as forerunner.

This means, in the first place, that his appearance marks the conclusion of the Old Covenant; coming from the Old Covenant, he is the first to cross the threshold of the New. To that extent, he is the fulfillment of the Old Covenant in its entirety, whose mission is exhausted in pointing toward Christ. However, John is the first to testify personally to the light, and his mission is therefore unequivocally beyond the threshold; it is a mission in the New Testament. God's charge to Moses and to the prophets of the Old Testament was always circumscribed, a limited mandate within righteousness. The mandate was proclaimed and could be carried out so that the obligation and its fulfillment coincided exactly. In the New Testament, the injunction given to John contains an unlimited demand: an absolute testimony to the light. The injunction is promulgated in love and (however hard it may be) in joy, for it is promulgated within the Son's mission. Everything about John's mission is characterized by love. That is why the injunction and its performance can never be squared: the order may be surpassed in the performance (because it is done in the grace of the Son), but those who have to carry it out know that the two can never truly correspond; obedience always lags behind the injunction. Nor will they ever know how far the performance is due to their own effort and how far (infinitely more) to the strength of the Lord's grace. The Father's gratitude is addressed primarily to the Son; his thanks to the witnesses are included therein. The relation of the witness to the Son is twofold, two-sided: the witness points away from himself toward the Son's light, deeply conscious of his insufficiency. But the more deeply he is convinced of being a useless servant, the more the Son gives him of his own light and mission and the more he draws the witness into the eternal movement from the Father and back to him—the more grace he gives him to administer and dispense to others.

It is significant that John, of his own accord, baptizes only in water but that his task is to baptize the Lord himself with that baptism that is the beginning and origin of all spiritual baptism. Starting with that baptism, John baptizes in the spirit and communicates the life of faith not only through the Word but also through the sacrament. It is furthermore significant that the Lord is conceived in Mary by the Holy Spirit and that John in his mother's womb receives the Spirit through Mary. The threads of the mission all pass through Mary's hands. God himself confers the mission, but Mary communicates something to it herself, something of her fruitfulness, of her living vitality. Christ's mission is eternally in God, but it was through his Mother's consent that it became an actual, human mission. In the same way, too, John is given his mission while still in his mother's womb, but it was through his contact with the Mother of God that it was awakened and given to him as a human mission.

Every mission is a mission in the Holy Spirit. If the Lord came into the world in order to reveal the Father, and if he was the revelation of the Father, this was by virtue of the Holy Spirit sent down upon him by the Father. The Holy Spirit is both the messenger of the mission and the mission itself. He is the missionary of the mission. On the one hand, he is the witness in God who testifies to the relation between Father and Son, the only one who can testify "impartially" to their eternal love and to the mystery of their separation on the Cross. On the other hand, as the Third in God, he is the eternal exchange and communication between Father and Son, the confidant of both, who transmits their love and is the messenger of love. That is why the Spirit is at the same time the witness to the glory that the Son has deposited in God—he makes it visible in faith—and to the mission given to the Son by the Father—in the form of the dove.

The Christian mission springs inspired from the Holy Spirit: it is alive, free, open—never closed or completed; it grows and flows on uninterruptedly and cannot be nailed down; in the course of being carried out, it grows richer and gives more generously and for that very reason makes more and more demands. The Holy Spirit is at work in the Son's mission; he is the life of love itself, the blood that pulsates in the Divinity. And because the Son fulfills his mission to the utmost limit, the Christian mission is, for us, an inexhaustible source, a perpetual beginning.

And finally, in the New Covenant the exceptional mission is a mission in the Holy Spirit, because it is not exhausted in the love between the Lord and his disciples. The disciple not only wants to carry out a particular work for the Lord to the very end, to do his will in a way that cannot be more closely defined, but demands that his work should resemble the Lord himself, like a woman who wants not only a child by the man she loves, but a child who resembles him, inherits his spirit, and realizes his plans. She wants to help spiritually to form the essence of the man from whom she passively conceives and whose fruit she bears. The Holy Spirit imparts the quality of sonship to the disciple's mission and gives it that mark in common with the Lord. Christ and Mary create in the Christian a loving faith, preparedness. Christ and the

Spirit transform him into active faith, which allows itself to be used as the instrument of the Lord, without asking where grace leads. He knows that his mission means living on the love of God, and that suffices for him.

THE WORD IN THE
SACRAMENTS

1:9. *The true light that enlightens every man was coming into the world.*

The light of the Word came into the world not only to shine in the universal darkness but also to enlighten and strike upon every single individual man. It accomplishes this end and reaches the individual through the *sacraments* and in no other way. The essential content of grace is faith, love, and hope, and this content is poured into the form of the sacraments; through them it is differentiated and molded into the grace of the Church.

Faith, love, and hope are a single river, without banks and without end, that flows from God and returns to God. They are one and formless, the life and light of grace. Now God himself is threefold, and as such his life has form. He is the God of order even in love, and that is why he gives us the life and light of his Word in a definite form. This form is the Church, which contains and dispenses the sacraments, the source of life and light, within a certain order.

The form is in no sense a subordinate consideration, subsequently imparted to the life: love for another never remains concealed in the private sphere of the I. The moment love appears, it concerns not only me but also Thou. Love being what it is, the Thou acquires certain "rights", the right to join in the dialogue. It has rights over the spirit and over the sphere of sex and life and in the cares of the lover. Similarly, man's love of God cannot remain a private, individual affair. In faith, love, and hope, the individual gives God rights over his existence and life. The one loved cannot live on love alone, on the mere assurance of love; this solitary love must really open out and surrender itself to become a gift. The sacraments are love objectified, and they preserve love from the danger of exhausting itself in a private and subjective world. That is why God desires the love between himself and man to have this form. The sacraments are the physical, sensual demonstration of the reality of the life of grace: of God's love for us and our love for him. It is the sacraments that make and keep love healthy, so that it always thirsts for more, not for the sake of augmenting itself (which would lead only to an egotistical attitude imprisoned in the I), but for the sake of belonging increasingly to God. Real vitality springs from the sacraments; they are the source where love bubbles up fresh, clear, and, as it were, naïve; the spring whence love is nourished is the center of exchange where the community of love lives and pulsates. The sacraments are the form and place of love.

And lastly, it can be seen from the sacramental form of grace that the sacraments are destined for sinners. Sin consumes the life of faith, love, and hope. From man's point of view, it seems as though sin first of all extinguished love, then faith, and finally hope. But seen by God, it is hope that goes first; God takes hope away first as being the basic thing; and man lives on in an empty hope, which is no longer hope at all but an empty husk, and without noticing what is missing. He imagines that sin has merely shut off the view and that everything behind the screen remains unaltered and unaffected, that when he needs it again he has only to stretch out a hand for the hope deposited there. But seen by God, hope is the one thing that cannot be stored away. It is then that the sacraments intervene and enter the life that has been destroyed.

Life, the pure life that flows like an unending bond from God to man and back again to God, is marked by the sacraments, offering man fresh starting points. The sacraments form the definite points at which grace can enter in again, the points onto which man can hold in the confusion of sin. They give the sinner a handle he can feel; they are banisters for him to lean upon, and with their help he can stand upright again. If there were no such thing as sin, or if there were nothing but sin, there would be no sacraments. They are auxiliaries in our transition from a forlorn condition in the world where we are lost to the life of God.

Now, although the sacraments give form and particularity to eternal life and in this sense seem to limit and contain it, grace is nevertheless in them as it might be in an overflowing vessel. So little do they resemble a measured dose of grace that each—in its way—breaks through our human limits. For one thing, they contain all grace in such a way that it is always infinitely greater than our expectation and our capacity to receive it. And then they are enriched by being dispensed. The more grace flows through them, the fuller the vessel out of which grace flows. The more grace flows through them, the more grace there is to flow. For the more grace God can dispense, the more manifest his magnanimity becomes. And love, after all, feeds upon love. Furthermore, the grace that God bestows, however feebly it may be received by man, is always fruitful. For the grace that works in us no more belongs to us than its product; it belongs to God. Grace increases grace; it is the most fruitful thing there is. It is quite simply the creativeness of God that created the real world out of nothing.

The paradox of the sacraments is that they are at the same time the forms of grace, grace particularized and differentiated, as well as grace that knows neither bounds nor limits; on the contrary, they dispense an overflowing grace.

This may also be seen from the fact that sacramental grace infinitely surpasses the moment of its reception, working on throughout the whole life of the recipient and even, in certain circumstances, beyond his life, in the life of his children and his children's children or among those with whom he comes in contact. This superfluity also explains how the different sacramental graces are mutually contained within each other, prepare the recipient for one another, increase one another, and flow in a single stream without losing their sacramental individuality. This paradox makes it clear that the sacraments themselves are love; for love is always quite concrete, definite, and particular and at the same time infinite and overflowing. That is true of all love: of sensual love, which manifests its fruitfulness in procreation; and still more so of caritative love, where kindness and helpfulness awaken further kindness and further helpfulness. The sacraments participate, then, in the essence of love. They are the light of love shining visibly in the world. And the unity of particularity and superfluity is visible in each one of them.

Baptism makes us into children of God even before we awaken to reason. It is an infinite gift and an infinite obligation. We ought by right to enter this existence of ours as sinners, but God wipes away our guilt. We ought to spend our lives wiping away our guilt in the eyes of God, but God not only cancels our debt but also gives us an advance of grace in its stead, and for the rest of our lives we can draw on the surplus. He takes away the debt that we inherit from our forefathers and in its place creates in us an infinite debt of gratitude. He gives us a reserve of grace that not even repeated sin can exhaust. God will always forgive the sinner who returns to him in the name of baptismal grace. And by virtue of that grace, which remains with him even in sin, the sinner can always demand the forgiveness of God. For baptismal grace, the effect of which lasts throughout life, is not consumed bit by bit. After all our needs and requirements have been satisfied, there remains a surplus of grace. It is the inexhaustible source of supply that God gives his children on the road of life. It gives the sinner in the court of judgment the right to be judged more leniently. The sins of the baptized may well be heavier than those of the pagan who knows nothing of the grace of sonship, but, by virtue of baptism, they can be more easily forgiven. For baptism is the pledge of God's mercy.

But baptismal grace is never limited to the baptized. The child receives it without being able to give his consent, though the reception of grace always implies a previous agreement. So someone speaks for the child and acknowledges that he belongs to God and not to himself. Those who do so—usually the parents and the godparents—participate in the grace given. The decision to baptize a child and bring him up a Christian bears with it a grace usually ignored by the parents, a grace that forms one with the baptismal grace of their child. They give their child to God, and through them he becomes God's possession: and the unity of that active and passive gift is answered by God in the grace of baptism, which passes whole and undivided to the baptized child and those taking part and bestows upon them a new relationship in God.

And insofar as she takes part in this acknowledgment, the whole Church receives grace from each baptism, a grace from which there proceeds a sort of unity and spiritual relationship between the baptized child and the

Church and, so, between all Christians. And this is where
the grace of baptism involves obligations. The individual
who is baptized becomes the administrator of the divine
treasure entrusted to him, which he has to administer in
a divine sense. And where God is concerned, administra-
tion signifies giving. Baptismal grace implies among other
things that it must be handed on to others by those who
possess it, if only because giving itself leads to God. For
every time a man dips into his treasure in order to communicate something of it to others, he is obliged to recollect
that it is not his own, but God's. He must give in such a
way that in giving he fulfills the will of God and so that
it is done in the name of God. The moment he goes to
his treasure because another man needs it, he will see the
other man's need with new eyes and begin to see it with
the eyes of God. Formerly, perhaps, he may have thought
that being in possession of so much he could help in a
human way. Now he knows that God alone can enable
him to help others with the treasure deposited in him. And
so whenever it overflows on to our neighbor, baptismal
grace leads us back to its beginning and origin in God.

Baptism does not prevent us from falling back into sin, but
it guarantees us the forgiveness of God in that event. The
grace of confession is therefore contained in the grace of
baptism. *Confession* gives us the possibility of always being
able to return to God from sin. Its particularity consists in
the first place in its being an entirely personal occurrence
between God and the soul. There is a definite relation between contrition and self-accusation, on the one side,
and forgiving grace, on the other. This particular grace
is placed in the hands of the recipient as in no other sacrament. He can receive it very largely at his own discre-
tion. He himself can restore order, receiving from God

the power to re-form the life he had forfeited, to regulate it once again, and to canalize the river of his life anew. In consequence, the grace of confession is strongly marked and very individual.

Man comes before God with the darkness of his sins and asks for the light of grace. It is a personal meeting, which signifies, in the first instance, the meeting of darkness and light, of minus and plus. The surplus of grace given here, as everywhere, is not a sort of advance as in baptism, but enters forthwith into the personal life of the penitent. The grace of confession creates purity and gives man strength to hold on to that purity. Whereas the continuity of baptism throughout life lies in baptism itself, the continuity of confession lies in Communion. But if that were the whole meaning of confession, it would remain a purely private affair between God and the soul. That is ruled out by the very nature of grace, which is always that of the Church: that is to say, communal, social. The sinner who comes to confess his sins before God comes to confess his own sins, and this personal aspect is so clear that he is utterly debarred from weakening or even excusing the reality of his sins with a side-glance at other sinners. Whatever his sin may be, however formed, it is always unforgivable and frightful. And for that very reason, his sin embraces the sin of the whole world; his sin is in communion, as it were, with universal sin and with its first author and father, the devil. It is not merely the individual sinner who stands before God, but the child of the devil, a member of the community of Satan. And, similarly, the priest who hears confession and gives absolution represents the voice of God, which is all-embracing and forgives the individual only in the context of the unending act of forgiveness and the entire scheme of redemption. In confession, the penitent is absorbed into the Lord's scheme of redemption.

And it is only within the scheme of redemption that the terrible contradiction with which he comes before God can be effaced: the contradiction between his sin and the purity of God.

While the penitent begs God for help, God leads him through a sort of shortened form of the sufferings of Christ. The way lies through repentance and contrition, past one's sins and tepidity up to the experience of judgment in the confession of one's sins and on to the sight of heaven in absolution received; from sorrow over oneself to an equally acute joy and thankfulness over God's goodness: such is the way of every confession, in which God immerses us for a moment in the sufferings of his Son, and this brief (though not necessarily superficial) intimation of the Passion broadens out to become a more than personal event. It is an event that happens to and in the Church.

Reconciliation with God is always reconciliation with the Church. The sinner is always to some extent outside the Church. Even if he is not excommunicated, he is outside the center of the Church, in which is the perfect purity of the Lord. Confession means being led back to that center. In some cases from a great distance, in others from close by. Though the distance plays no sort of part at the moment of return. The only thing that matters is to know that having been outside one is once again within and that this happens through the Lord and his Cross.

The aim of confession, perhaps the most personal sacrament, is that the believer should reenter the Church, as it were impersonally, and become a member of the community among other members. He certainly has the duty to confess to God, but also to the Church. That is why the grace of confession is also a communal grace. This grace is given in part to the penitent for his own; in part it is mysteriously allotted for the purification and enlightening of the community. For while there is a communion in sin, there is also, in a far higher sense, a communion in grace. And the fewer definite and precise sins a man has to confess, the more he is in duty bound to confess the communal, anonymous guilt of all the members of the Church. And the Church, equally, has the right to demand that the sinner, particularly if he is weighed down with grave sins, should purify himself through confession, so that the Church should not be sullied in her entirety by the presence of a sinful member. Through confession, the Christian is led away from himself into the life of the community. That is why confession ought to be the very opposite of meditation on one's sins. The priest must indeed know what he has to judge, and the penitent what he has to confess. But the point of confession is neither sin nor the confession of sin, but simply and solely the grace of the Lord. Confession should consist solely in the opening of the heart to grace; and the measure of confession is the degree to which one's heart is opened. The mark of a good confession is not the recognition of one's sin as such or the courage to have confessed "even that"; for in confession, too, there is a *noli-me-tangere*; one turns away from sin so as to see nothing but grace. Otherwise, confession would not be participation in the way of the Lord, which leads back to the Father through the Cross. The way back to the center of the Church is a return to the center of the Father. Into the burning light of the Father. Whether the sinner comes from the outer darkness or was already in the light, he will certainly be consumed and burned by the inmost light.

A considerable time passes in the life of a Christian child between baptism and confession. As a rule, the Christian receives baptism unknowingly; confession he receives as one already in the light of knowledge. Between the two lies the period of awakening, when knowledge begins. It is the time of the *guardian angel*, of instruction, when the Christian life unfolds within the Church. It is also the time when the first mistakes are made and the first false steps are taken, though they are not at first serious. This is thanks to the guardian angel, in whose company the child lives and who protects him in a special manner until he reaches the age of reason. A child examines his conscience in the presence of the angel. He can distinguish between good and evil and knows that some things are not allowed. But he does not see the implications and consequences of good and evil. What he cannot see is left to the angel, who inspires the child to ask forgiveness for what he has done, at the same time strengthening his naïveté and, above all, not explaining sin. The child is simply led away from the dangerous path, and no light is thrown on the meaning of evil. The guardian angel is an artist in concealment and deflection, who extracts good from evil and gets the best out of the good. So much can be destroyed by words and explanations. And in this he resembles a good confessor, who points the right way without drawing attention to sin. All subsequent confessions retain something of this grace. In the afterlife one continues to beg forgiveness for one's sins like a child and to include everything that one does not understand and cannot view as a whole. The whole Christian life is sustained by a particular fundamental humility that belongs to the period between baptism and confession.

In baptism and confession, the special, particular aspect of grace is very clear, and it is all the more necessary to stress the other aspect, the unlimited, open, and overflowing aspect. In *Communion*, in contrast, the unlimited aspect is at first almost the only one apparent. In baptism and confession, there exists a certain relationship between the sin wiped out and the grace given. Both are connected with a precise view of the relation between sin and grace. In spite of the preponderance of grace, some sort of balance and proportion are preserved between the divine and human partners.

In Communion, on the contrary, there is neither balance nor proportion. It is a purely one-sided prodigality. One receives the Lord for no other reason than that he gives himself without reserve. The question of our worth is ruled out. The only thing required of the recipient is his readiness to receive with an open heart. Preparation is of course necessary. But the real preparation for Communion is confession; then it is complete. And if a man has sinned after confession, then he must at least confess his sins to God, even if he does not need to confess them to the Church. This act of purification precedes Communion, happens before Communion, but is not an act proportioned to the gift of the Lord in Communion. The grace of Communion is sheer overflowing, incompatible with any form of reckoning. Man can only let himself be filled to overflowing by it.

Communion is the overflowing answer of God's love to the barely indicated love of man. It puts a complete end to accountancy because at its center is the mystery of substitution. Through the grace of the Son, we really assume his grace; it is given to us so that we stand before the Father clothed in the Son's grace. The moment we have the Son's Body in us, he sees the Son in us, and in his eyes we are the Son's brothers. For this reason, Communion is the occasion for the Father to give us his grace in unlimited measure. He forgets that we are sinners and regards us as his sons. He loves his Son to such a degree that for love of him he receives us as sons. He does this out of love for the Son, to whom in his prodigal gift of himself he gave the grace to be not only the giver but also the receiver. For in Communion, the Lord wishes to be and to feel himself a brother among brothers and to give himself so that in doing so he is given by us. A man who has communicated is no longer the man he was before. Not by reason of the external act of communicating, but because the Lord transforms him (though he does not know how) from a worthless creature into a King's son. It is just as though the Son of God had permission from his Father to wander about the highways and byways and take his friends, ragged and dirty as they are, into his Father's house and introduce them as his friends. The moment he does so, they are friends of the house, transformed into companions worthy of him. Such is the grace of Communion, which overflows all bounds.

Although in its effect it works upon our inmost self, it is nevertheless impersonal. It flows on beyond our own person without our being able to set bounds to it. The Eucharist is simply there, in the Church; it is Real Presence and is given in some superpersonal way to all who desire it. It is not only effective when it is distributed. It works in the Church as a whole and in the individual believer. Everyone who is in the Church and sees the Real Presence is affected by it. It is also received when it is only adored. It is no less in its effect at evening devotions than in morning Communion. The grace of Communion simply flows on, filling the whole Church with its light. In those who are unable to receive it as an outward sacrament, it works directly and inwardly. The gift of the Lord is the same and belongs to the same kind of gift as his gift of himself, which is unlimited and superpersonal. Communion makes possible the Communion of Saints. No one can or may communicate for himself, not even in the sense in which he is baptized for himself.

The transition from confession to Communion is an immediate one. Confession opens the way to the Lord: the Lord comes into his own house. Everything is prepared. The Lord in us awaits the Lord. The house does not need to be prepared by us: it *is* ready. We *are* pure. In confession, the Lord gives us the possibility of coming before him as *his* creatures. Confession removes the importance of sin and of the sinners we are. Unworthiness no longer plays a part. The infinite disproportion falls away. Nor is there any relation between the frequency of confession and Communion. Various factors regulate the frequency of confession, though it must not be so frequent as to lead the individual to busy himself with his own sin more than with the grace of God. Nor should it be too seldom, for he should constantly renew the experience of opening his heart to the Lord through the priest, of hearing the voice of God that bursts him open. Whether we confess our highly uninteresting sins daily or weekly or monthly does not much matter. However, it is not a matter of indifference how often we experience the purity of the Lord, who touches us in absolution. Nor is spiritual direction a reason for frequent confession. In confession the priest is only an official instrument, the representative of the Lord.

Where Communion is concerned, the frequency of its reception is judged by other standards. The Lord is the nourishment of our souls, and it is good to receive Communion often and even daily. It is our primary food (the justification of the law of fasting), a nourishment that comes from above, from the Father, and leads us to the Father. It cannot be digested in the way that food is digested by the body; it leaves no dross behind, but integrates us in the Lord, opening us to his mission. The Eucharist lives on in us as his mission. This mission must, however, be listened to afresh and differently at each Communion. The soul never knows how the Lord is going to give himself. Each time the soul receives the Lord, its expectation must be new, fresh, undimmed, unpaled by habit and custom. That is the spiritual equivalent of fasting, the emptiness that true Communion presupposes. If the place in the soul set aside for the Lord is cluttered up with habit and custom, Communion will be robbed of its fruitfulness. Then a less frequent Communion may be indicated, so as to receive the Lord with renewed vitality.

Just as confession was planted in baptism, so too is the grace of *confirmation*, which appertains to the grace of baptism; it liberates and builds up what baptism awakens in the child. It is the sacrament of maturity and ripeness. The grace of confirmation consists in the bestowal by the Church of the Church's Holy Spirit; that is to say, it expands faith into full membership of the Church, deepening it into a realization that the Church is not merely an institution, but life. It bestows the knowledge that in that institution, the Church, the Holy Spirit is alive. Confirmation strengthens and secures everything that is alive in the Church and consequently the other sacraments, too. It is ordered entirely toward the other sacraments; it is the invisible and omnipresent salt that permeates and preserves the entire life of the Church. It is a relative, not an absolute sacrament. It brings the individual to the Church and does so by making him "of age" and proclaiming his majority. It makes him capable of judging for himself within the Church and of looking at things with the eyes of the Church. It bestows a sort of discernment upon him in matters relating to the Church and gives him the right to a voice in the community. The fact that confirmed members of the Church have a voice in the community and may claim the right to use it ought to be more clearly in the minds of the Church's leaders.

The distinguishing mark of the grace of confirmation is, moreover, what makes it universal and overflowing. It explodes and bursts open the personal life of the believer and obliges him to become a responsible member of the community. He must get to know the Church, of which he is a living member, better. He has outgrown the milk of passive learning and must go on to the solid food of self-education and continue his education in spiritual matters. He can no longer regard the Church simply as a completed Tradition and a fixed institution. He must feel the life and growth of the Church in everything and take part in it. The Church has a right to ask that he should be a useful member of the community, and his private life should be open toward the life of the Church. The grace of confirmation opens the minds of those who receive it to an ever-growing knowledge of the unity of spirit and institution, the unity of Christian freedom and obedience to the Church, and imparts an increasing willingness to be at her service and so to embody that unity. As long as the Christian is a minor in regard to the Church, he enjoys the privilege of playing, as it were, with the Church's means to grace, fitting them into his own childish, personal plans. But once he has outgrown childhood, the norm of his life is not his personal piety but the Catholic Church. He ought no longer to follow his whims or behave eccentrically, but renounce some of his personal preferences for the sake of peace, unity, and conformity in love; he ought to represent the Church.

Confession is no longer quite the same thing after confirmation. The confession may be outwardly the same; the failures of one who is confirmed, who has the Holy Spirit in him and the responsibility involved, are much more serious. He is no longer a child; he ought to know what he is doing. And finally, since confirmation is the gateway to mature life in the Church, it is a preparation for the two particular forms of life within the Church: the priesthood and marriage.

Ordination consecrates those who receive the sacrament and dedicates them as official administrators of grace. The grace of the priesthood consists in effecting a sort of fusion between what is personal in a man and the official of the Church, so that all that is personal is absorbed in the office, while the office colors all that is personal.

The particular quality of the grace of ordination is first of all apparent outwardly in the special authority and function of the priesthood; at the same time, what is special to the sacrament is a mysterious infinity, an immense surplus. This does not consist primarily in the fact that the priest receives a sort of personal reserve of grace in addition to the grace of his office (by virtue of which he is able to carry out his ministry worthily) but in the fact that his personal self becomes the property of the Church. The personal grace he receives flows immediately into the treasury of the Church. And this treasure, in its turn, is open to the priest, in such a manner that he can make it accessible to others. The special power of the blessing at a priest's first Mass is due, not to the private grace given to him, but to the fact that he has access for the first time to the Church's superpersonal treasury of grace. His ministry becomes personal in the same degree as all that is personal in him is poured into the ministry: he can give himself in everything that he communicates: he dispenses at the same time the substance of the Church and his own substance. For he bears the impress of the Church. That distinguishes him from the laity. And in giving himself to God, he becomes a gift to the community.

The sacrificial character of the sacraments is particularly pure and visible in Holy Orders. In baptism, the individual offers his own freedom for the good of the Church; in confession, he offers his sinfulness and "appearances" (for to the priest at least he sacrifices the appearance of being a "respectable man"); and in the same way the priest offers his whole personal existence to the Lord and the community and, thus, comes close to the Lord, who offers himself in the Host. And if the sacrifice of the whole community is called for in the Mass, it is the priest who has to represent the sacrifice personally and officially. It is by virtue of this sacrifice alone that he receives the grace to increase the grace of God. It is also by virtue of this sacrifice that he is enriched; every confession heard purifies him; every Communion given enriches him, for the Lord always pierces him through, working and speaking through him. But in giving himself at the same time to the community, he allows it to participate in his priesthood. To this extent, there is an analogy to the priesthood in the community: there is a graduated approach to the grace of the priesthood that rises from the lowest step of purely passive reception up to the highest step of giving oneself, with the priest. And on that frontier lies the special sacrifice made by those laymen who, encouraged as a rule by a priest, have learned a true and unlimited devotion to their neighbors. As a result of the poverty and selflessness that belong to this particular sacrifice, the superfluity of grace that it produces is transferred entirely to the community. It is woman above all who participates in this invisible and hidden priesthood, standing as she does next to the priest, like Mary next to John beneath the Cross.

The special distinction of the sacrament of *marriage* consists in the Christian consecration of the natural spiritual and corporal relation between man and woman. And that is precisely what makes it unlimited and overflowing. It does not take effect in a single subject but, from the first,

affects a living unity of I and Thou. It is received, not by
two individual people, but by a new community. And it is
promulgated to this community, given indivisibly to man
and wife insofar as they are a new unity in God.

Up till now, the circle of grace went from God to the
individual, to the Church, and to God; here it goes from
God to the community of marriage, to the child, and
through them to the Church and to God. In other cases,
the superfluity of grace benefits the Church as an already
existing institution. In this case, it is given to the family
itself as a cell of the Church. Personal grace benefits the
community only as the result of a sacrifice, but the grace
given to the family flows on of itself to the child. That is,
of course, a source of danger: the family can be regarded
as a closed community, whereas it must always be open
to the community and the Church. It is easier to con-
vince the individual that he, a sinner, must sacrifice his
self. The family, in contrast, is a sort of ideal in the name
of which one tends to withhold the sacrifice. Parents easily conceal a collective egoism beneath the virtue of pro-
viding for the future and behind a love that exhausts itself
within the family. That is the closed circle that is broken
open by the sacramental grace of marriage. The essence
of this grace is that it enables one to love the child in God
and God in the child; it opens out the earthly sphere of
love in order to introduce God and, with God, of course,
the Church.

The grace of marriage is, of course, primarily the sanc-
tification of the life of married people, for it bestows what
the one possesses on the other and makes it fruitful for
him. The faith and love and sacrifice of the one sanctifies
both. And further, at each hour of every day, they have
the possibility of being two, gathered together in God's
name, so that in accordance with his promise the Lord will

be present. But all this occurs simply and solely as a result of the first Yes they say to one another in God and in which they mutually abandon and leave each other to God. And the mystery of the natural as of the supernatural fruitfulness of Christian marriage is grounded in that mutual Yes, given in God. The consent of husband and wife in Christian marriage includes consent to the child, because they consent to love as grace given by God and fruitful through God. The child in this case is no longer the apparently fortuitous result of love between two people, which is what children are when love is regarded as purely human and used as an impulse. That love is imprisoned within itself and is only fortuitously burst open by the fact of the child. The child raises a subsequent and quite new problem to this enclosed love, which must take thought before achieving an attitude to the new factor. The child of a Christian marriage, on the contrary, was affirmed from the beginning as the fruit of God's grace and taken up into marriage as something belonging to God and the Church, something given to the parents and not entirely at their disposal—a source of new strength for their love rooted in God.

The mutual love of husband and wife is, on the one hand, so wide that God alone can fill it and, on the other side, so much the gift of grace that it bears with it the promise of fruitfulness, a promise that in fact remains entirely with God and is not in the hands of the parents. One expression of this fact is that parents can never be certain of conceiving a child; the act of begetting children is a mystery and takes place in confidence. The fulfillment of their love has been placed in the hands of God, and they thus carry out the will of God as expressed in nature. They recognize in him the Lord of the fruitfulness of love. One cannot (and must not) reckon upon children, because one cannot measure grace:

children are an expression of the freedom of fruitfulness and are therefore a symbol of the Holy Spirit.

Man, woman, and child are a unity, according to God's plan; and even in the concrete instance of a particular family, they are a unity of thought and willed by God. The woman is intended by God for this particular man, and this particular child is reserved to them. And so in God's plan the child is the unity of the parents, even though, in the physical world of time, he merely slumbers potentially within them, who bear him within them separately. Potentially the *one* child is already present in both of them. He forms their potential unity. In begetting and birth, they bring forth the child as a real unity by surrendering what made them one in God and realizing that unity in the form of the child given them by God, thus taking back their unity into the grace of marriage.

This unity was sent forth that it might be realized; it was surrendered to God, and that is why it is the parents' duty to allow their unity to become fruitful in God, giving the fruit to God. That means that they must give their child to the Church and to the community of those belonging to God. Being a child of Christian parents, and therefore the child of grace, he has a right to baptism. Both graces include one another mutually: thus Christian marriage is unity in God, and one cannot properly speak of Christian marriage having two different ends as in the case of natural marriage.

It is only in natural marriage that the child can be considered separately and apart, as outside the personal love of husband and wife. In Christian marriage, husband and wife belong to one another in God: the child is included in their faith, love, and hope—the child that God may give them. God may reserve the child for himself by giving him a vocation either to the priesthood or to a religious order;

and insofar as the parents have already consented in their Yes to allow the child to go the way of God, the sacrifice demanded of them is in the beginning. God does not necessarily give husband and wife children. It would not be grace if it were given necessarily.

It is because the blessing of children is left open that Christian marriage remains open toward the Church. Every Christian marriage is blessed by God and is fruitful in him, whether through the blessing of children or the blessing of sacrifice. If God chooses the second alternative, the spiritual fruitfulness of marriage is increased and widened out invisibly so that it flows into the whole community. The natural and supernatural fruitfulness of marriage and of the Church form an inseparable unity. A vocation to the priesthood or to the religious life may lead to the extinction of a family but to the beginning of unending fruitfulness in the Church.

The Church, too, knows the double meaning and mystery of blessing, either as fruitfulness or as sacrifice, for God decides whether a community is to be rich and fruitful or, humanly speaking, sterile. Whether the blood of martyrs flowers in the miracle of a new Christianity or whether the persecuted Christianity of a whole country disappears, seemingly without fruit. In this mystery, the Church and marriage are one. But their mutual relationship must not be understood as though the fruitfulness of marriage gave the Church children and as though the fruitfulness of the Church fed upon that of marriage. The fruitfulness of the Church is fed by God alone. Christian marriage is fruitful for the Church only when it is made fruitful by God himself, when husband and wife are consumed in God, giving their very substance, their possibilities to God, and when this gift takes the form of begetting and conceiving.

The Church herself was born in the death of Christ, when he gave his substance and power into the complete darkness of God, unable any longer to see its effect. In his words: "Father, into your hands I commit my spirit", the Lord becomes the image and symbol of generation. He forgets himself utterly, gives himself so completely out of his own hands that he gives his Spirit, not back to the Spirit of God, but into the hands of God. Every Christian marriage must open itself to the mystery of the Cross in order that the I and its personal substance should be liberated through the family in a sacrifice of itself with Christ, in the Church, and through the Church in the Father.

The light that came into the world to enlighten every man shines upon him as he leaves this world to return to the Father. *Extreme unction* leads the completed life back into the unending river of faith, love, and hope. All the sacraments lead man to God; they reorientate him. But the anointing of the sick is the final and essential reorientation. Confession and Communion can be received at will; one can help to orientate oneself. But in the last sacrament, one is led. Even when one receives extreme unction freely, it remains of its essence something brought from outside. In no other instance is the priest so independent; it is he who dispenses the sacrament unconditionally in the name of God.

Extreme unction is the transition from a personal, self-directed life into the community of the saved, over which it disposes. Even in the other sacraments, one always surrenders oneself to a higher, invisible law, however free and independent one is: the measure of one's reception or failure to receive is no longer in one's hands. In the very act of receiving, one is received rather than receiving. This law becomes absolute in extreme unction. Man can participate only to the extent of making his spiritual testament; he turns away from all that has been and holds himself in readiness to be at the sole disposal of God. In extreme unction, the Christian's death is placed at the Lord's service, that death which the Lord tasted, whose bitterness he drank; and the dying have only to repeat the words: Father, into your hands I commit my spirit. The grace of extreme unction, too, overflows its form: enveloped in its superfluity, the anointed appear before God clothed as the brothers of Christ. But its superfluity also envelops the family and the community; they receive it consciously through the edification of the sacrament itself and unconsciously in that here, where life is at an end, from an earthly point of view, one and all may find a new beginning. For dying in God is always fruitful.

All seven sacraments together form *the light of the world*. They are the light, because in them God's light becomes accessible to the world. They are the light of God for the further reason that, although particularized and distinct, they possess the all-pervading, radiating quality of the light, which is mysteriously omnipresent and cannot be obscured. Baptism is present throughout the Christian life precisely because it is a definite action in time and space. The Lord in the Eucharist is omnipresent in the Church, and through the Church in the world, because his presence possesses the definite, particular, and Real Presence of the Host. This aspect of the light of the sacraments shines in the darkness of those who receive them.

The world and the Church do not receive the sacraments as they should be received. They adopt them as a precautionary measure and use them as a safety device, when each sacrament really releases a safety catch and takes us out of "safety" into God. They are received as though man were completing an action upon God, whereas of course they are the action of God upon man. And yet there are some who receive them and who, through the sacraments, are born of God, and everyone who receives them receives with them the demand of light, that there may be more light. Those who receive a sacrament must see that others receive it. If a man is the only person in Church to receive Communion, he is in duty bound to see that others communicate. The obligation is one of the consequences of the shining of the light, for the more it shines, the more intense its light. For the content of the sacraments is love, which is always an indivisible unity of love of God and for one's neighbor. That is why it is not the invisible sacramental grace alone but the visible act itself that enters and works in the community. The supernatural grace is of such a kind that one part of it becomes the natural power of communication. The invisible works itself out in the visible. Neither sphere can be separated from the other. Just as the washing of the feet was an act of grace and a most visible act of natural love, so too is the action of man, of priest and layman, of dispenser and receiver: it is an act both human and divine, natural and supernatural, within the sacramental sphere of the Church. Those who participate in this action know quite well that there is no question of a fusion of God and man. The disjunction between the sinners they are and the children of God whom they become through sacramental grace is never more clear than in the reception of the sacraments. For when God restores unity in us, he simultaneously emphasizes the disjunction; only it is no longer a tragic condition because in the unity restored to us we once again return to the disparity expressed in our adoration and in our mission.

THE WORD REJECTED

1:10–11. *He was in the world, and the world was made through him, yet the world knew him not. He came to his own home and his own people received him not.*

The Lord came into the world and with him grace, Church, sacraments, and mission. All that he brought, all that he is and does and says, the whole stupendous preparation, his offer and his armament, that is the world he made. For the reference in the text is not to the old creation, which certainly was God's, but to the new, essential, and final creation, which took place when he came into the world.

When a man becomes a Christian, it happens simply and solely through the Lord's love. Creative love makes him what he is. Only one thing is needed to complete the new creation: that man should not refuse grace. He must let himself be taken up into God's creation in order to become part of the new creation. Everything is there; everything is ready: grace, faith, love, hope, and mission; the new life is prepared in every detail; the framework and armament are complete; the spring of a new life is flowing. The world that leads an unreal life could have found real life within the new framework, found its true creation. Like a shapeless lump of dough in a mold, it had only to let itself receive the new form. But that grain of agreement is precisely what is wanting. The world refuses to correspond to the new form. It does not want to be what it was intended to be: it refuses to be the world of the Word and refuses to belong to the Word. It will not respond or correspond to creative grace. That is why the whole new creation runs like a machine that has nothing to work upon.

As the world well knows, the new creation involves being transformed by God. But what it does not realize is that the transformation is accompanied by supreme joy, a joy that, though spiritual, does not send the flesh away empty. It sees only the negative aspect: death and the renunciation of everything it loves and clings to. In the eyes of the world, the one and only good is whatever pleases *it*, gives *it* joy, is agreeable to *it*; it looks at everything from that one standpoint. In the new creation, the center of gravity is transposed into God. The weight is shifted. The true good is God, and God is true joy. But the world does not want it so. For the world is flesh, nothing but flesh, whereas the new creation is spirit in which the flesh, too, finds its proper place.

So *the world knew him not*. One cannot recognize God as long as one stands between one's I and God. As long as the center of gravity is in one's I, one sees God only through that I; God is regarded as a means to the satisfaction, cruder or more refined, of one's I and is included for that reason in one's calculations and plans. Do that, and you cannot know God. God is love, and only *those* who love recognize God. A God who existed only for my sake would be no God. It is also possible to use God as an *Ersatz*. When a man loses what is dearest to him, the one thing he lived for, he is left with a great void in his soul, and in his emptiness he calls to God. He wants God to fill the void. If the need is real, it may lead to God and to the knowledge of God. But it may equally be that the God involved is only a passing *Ersatz*, to be forgotten the moment something worldly comes to fill the void. And in that case, too, the world fails to recognize him. Whenever God is just a function of the I, he remains unknown, even if he is the function of a religious need. For man is quite capable of imagining a God to satisfy his religious needs, in the same way that bread satisfies his hunger or another person satisfies his desires. A God of that kind is paid a sort of tax; he is allotted a precisely defined, limited place in life, and he is allowed to occupy the little void one has prepared for him, with the proviso that in certain circumstances it may have to be curtailed. To receive God in that way is really a form of ignorance.

This nonrecognition of God is better described as refusal or rejection. Men do not receive God because they have no desire for him. They desire only what they make and shape themselves. They renounce everything above their heads, the pursuit of which requires that they should be enlarged and expanded. They do the same in all love: at first they seem willing enough to expand in every direction (in marriage, for example); but as soon as the demand grows serious, they draw back. As long as men approach God with their own standards, their own weights and measures, their own demands, one cannot really say that they receive God. For to receive God means to make room for God—whatever he may be or bring. It may only be a call to be prepared, a vague, indefinite, and indefinable demand; in contrast, it may be a visible and intelligible task; it may be a single action or just one word to be spoken. But even then, the individual must be ready for everything, for the whole, for all that follows, for that which cannot be seen or foreseen. If he were prepared for only one task, he would not be receiving God, for in order to receive him, one must be ready for everything. Even for the background that one cannot see and never will see. Nowhere is it so true that if one gives one's word one must give one's whole self, body and soul. It is hardly ever possible to see from the start all that God is to mean to one. God asks for blind confidence; to receive him is not to refuse oneself. Someone who offered a friend in need all the money he had on him would not be much of a friend if he were saying to himself: "Let's hope he won't take too much." He ought to be sorry he has not got more to offer. When God takes everything from a man, it is because he needs everything.

To receive God means to give oneself to God, even if our gift consists only in offering him our darkness so that his light may shine in it. The light itself sets no limits to its radiance. The limit can be set only by the darkness that receives it. Those who receive the light must be ready to let the light shine through them without setting any limit to its power; they must be ready to correspond more and more both to the gifts and to the demands of God's love.

Once open to the light, man may ask God to claim him more essentially and more profoundly. But on one condition only, on condition he does not refuse the first small act that God demands of him. Man's sorrow at not being able to offer God more is not infrequently due to the pride that imagines itself made for better things. But one's capacity to receive God is not the measure of one's mission, nor is it even the sum of everything in us that could be transformed to God's use. The only standard is God's need—though man is not debarred from offering himself more and more, in all humility.

The world, which *did not know* the Lord, consists of those who reject him from lack of vision and insight. *His own* who *knew him not* are those who know of him and have heard of him but knowingly and calculatingly close their minds to him. Nowadays most men have heard of him somehow or other. But they close their minds from the outset to the content of the Word of God. They reject him even before they have heard his Word. They have allowed themselves to be persuaded that the name and the concept of God are something negative: something that may reasonably enough be postponed till life is almost over, reserved for the beyond, or again, something perfectly irrelevant or even inimical to man both as individual and as community. Whole groups of people harden themselves and persist in a collective rejection of God. It is very difficult to stir an individual belonging to a closed group of this kind in such a way that God becomes a reality to him. One cannot produce the necessary shock either through human love or even by adjusting oneself to their situation and position in the community; for in all this the standards of value remain human: being myself the father of a family, I am not insensitive to the sufferings of my neighbors, and as I might find myself in the same predicament, I stand up for the rights of the union, etc. In the case of a collective rejection of God, only a convulsion that shakes the collective as a whole to its very foundations can produce a change, for it is only a great common need or catastrophe that changes social love, at bottom egotistic, into a selfless love of one's neighbor. Then, simultaneously, the way is opened to the reception of God.

But this world, the world that does not know the Lord and so rejects him, which rejects him and so does not know him, is *his own*. It is his own because he created it. It is also his because it was given him by the Father. A strange gift—which does not want to know or hear about him and is in deadly opposition to him. He is given the unconverted world, an impossible world that simply cannot be enjoyed. The Father gives the Son the vineyard and sends him to the vineyard, where the laborers think only of putting him to death. And by making him that gift, he hands him over to his enemies. That is the world that will know nothing of him and that the Son is to transform into a world that is really and inwardly his own. What he brings back to the Father is a world no longer without access to God, in which there is a mustard seed of hope that God may be received. Into which God, from now on, can penetrate, transforming it into his own. The world since the crucifixion is not the same as the world before the crucifixion.

His own, to whom he came, are those who ought to believe but do not. An indeterminate, ever-changing notion and therefore a mysterious one, simultaneously closed and open; a limited circle and at the same time a circle capable of unlimited expansion. In the first instance, "his own" are a limited circle. For the Lord came as a man into the world, came to a particular people at a particular time with a particular human mission corresponding to a particular circle of people, those who are addressed and touched by that mission. He comes as man and meets certain definite men. He comes with the human hope that these men— whom he meets in deed and in word, to whom he proclaims the Father's message, for whom and among whom he works miracles—will receive him as "his own". Without that hope, he would not have been man. And as man he believes that the effect produced on those whom he has moved will spread abroad to others living farther away and in other times. Every human mission has its limit, its particular aspect. The parish priest's mission corresponds to his parish, that of an apostle to the community of individuals specially addressed by the apostle's particular character, manner, and graces. Paul has his, so has Peter, and so has James, each allotted to them by God, corresponding to their office and the mission delivered to them. The Lord, too, has his own particular circle, and occasionally he speaks of it. Though it is plain that in his case (and through him, of course, the same is true of the apostles, the missionaries, the faithful) the limited circle opens out to the unlimited. Ultimately, "his own" are all men, for all belong to him, and all ought to reach faith through him. He is to die and rise again for all. The Father did not give him part of the world, but the whole world.

And so the circle of "his own" widens out to embrace the whole world, and he there sends "his own" out to the farthermost parts of the world. The limited circle to whom he is sent and to whom he sends his disciples in the first instance is simply the human point of contact necessary for an infinite movement. In order that the notion of "his own" should not remain vague, colorless, and abstract, so that we should see by example what it means to be spoken to and claimed by him, the movement without end has a starting point in a definite, limited circle. The relations within the limited circle are visible and human, and all the ordinary rules that govern spiritual relations, human confidence, friendship, and affection play their part. But as the circle expands, these visible and human traits disappear. The relation between the representative of God and "his own" does not disappear; on the contrary: the more formless the human relationship becomes, the less easy it is to grasp as a whole, the more precise it may become as a divine relationship. Not even an apostle can tell where the effect of his mission ends; the circle of those he draws into the invisible Kingdom of grace, and who are known to God alone here below, is just as real as the visible, human effect he produces.

And finally, "his own" are all those to whom the Lord has given something. They are his through his grace. And through it they are stamped with the seal that marks them as "his own". That does not exclude the possibility that they are at the same time those who have not received him. The Father gave them to him even before they had

made the decision to receive him or not to receive him.
And because the Father gave them to him, the Lord takes
them as "his own" into his possession. Some of them
know that they are his; others do not bother about it;
others do not even know it and reject him. They all carry
the Father's gift through life, though many are ignorant of
what they have in their pack. The Father gives them to the
Son without reference to their decision in the matter and
with the single thought that the Son's love for "his own"
will be stronger than their rejection of him, greater than
the whole tragedy and fiasco of the Word's being rejected.

Men always imagine that they belong to God on the
basis of their consent. But one may belong to the Lord
on other grounds: because of the redemption and without knowing it. Few of those who stood around the
Cross were aware that they were "his own". The majority rejected him. And yet, they were already touched by
him and belonged to him as "his own". That does not
alter the fact that one must receive the redemption and
fulfill the will of God. But the important thing is to be
possessed by the Lord, and that happened while we were
still sinners. For he chose us, not we him.

THE WORD RECEIVED

1:12. *But to all who received him, who believed in his name, he gave power to become children of God.*

There are indeed men who have received him, received him consciously. Among the first were his Mother, his foster father, the shepherds and kings, Simeon and Anna, Elizabeth and John, his disciples and many of the people.

Those who receive him consciously always do so in the same way: they give their consent to God rather than to the Son. They are men who know that God expects them to receive him. They may not know beforehand what receiving God means or how it happens or what the consequences will be. But they know that God awaits them, and they say Yes in such a way as to show their readiness to acknowledge all his further demands. But God's demand is faith in the Son, with the result that faith in the Son embraces all God's demands, indeed, all demands whatsoever. Those who are willing to make the leap from God to his Son, from the Father, who is presupposed if not known, to a Son whose existence could not be assumed and cannot be imagined (can anyone imagine God as man) are equally prepared, without knowing it, to say Yes to the ever-increasing demands of God in the Son.

In saying Yes to God, their minds and hearts are open to him unconditionally, and they allow themselves to be expanded by God till it becomes possible for them to receive his Son. This much they knew, that God would be greater than they themselves. They knew him only as the great unknown, a few of whose demands were known, though it was not their concern to worry over the demands of a God essentially unknown and offering so few points of contact to human understanding. It was easier to be a disciple of God than to become a disciple of Christ. But to those who want to belong to him, God now gives his Son. And from then on, Father and Son can no longer be separated. They wanted to believe in God, and now God demands that they believe in his Son. A more difficult thing by far: for in coming nearer to us, God, who was distant and inconceivable, becomes more inconceivable still. Moreover, since he came in human form, his demands are more distinct, more compelling, and impossible to overlook. It is easier to believe a miracle one is told about than a miracle one has seen for oneself. For the act of seeing throws us into direct contact with something that surpasses us.

The Father, then, directs us in our faith toward the Son: it is the Son we are to look to and look upon, follow and imitate. And in his turn, the Son speaks only of the Father, of how we are to contemplate the Father, listen to him, and be perfect like him. What is hidden first makes us aware of the visible, and then the visible directs us toward the hidden. Both paths are without end: the leap from the Father to the Son is not a leap from the infinite and the inconceivable to the finite and the conceivable, but, despite the Son's humanity, a leap nearer the inconceivable, always present behind the conceivable.

To receive God, then, means receiving the Son. The Yes said to the Son is at first simply uttered; my words fly outward as if to a being that is before me, above me, beside me. That is how we imagine the Son. We believe in the Son's *Name*. But our Yes is hardly uttered before it takes an altogether unexpected turn; it turns inward; it enters into us. The Son himself makes us aware that he is in us, hidden in our inmost I; so that the fact of his being hidden alters in character: he is hidden in us. At first we swear to follow and imitate the Son as one might swear on the flag or on one's word of honor, when suddenly everything becomes inward and personal. At first we receive the Son like a friend, but he enters the very heart of our being and drives out every other thought, even our self. The whole place belongs to him. One receives him as though he were great among other greatnesses, something definite and precise, for example a doctrine or a teaching one thinks one could represent, into which one could work one's way step by step. When suddenly the absolute is there, in my midst, something I cannot work upon, something, on the contrary, that works upon me. The choice that really was mine is the choice in which the Lord chose me. And because he chose me, he is my Lord. I thought I could surrender myself to him just as I pleased. But he drives me out of myself, expelling everything that does not serve his purpose.

As a result of being thus received and taken up by the Son, everything ceases to be clear, for my reception of him and his reception of me can no longer be clearly distinguished; the border between the one received and the one receiving is obliterated; one can no longer say who receives and who is received, where receiving begins and where being received ends. I am not a vessel receiving him as it might some content or other, for the content far surpasses the container; the vessel becomes an unimportant adjunct to the content. And what is true of the individual is of course true of the community. It is no longer the community that receives the Lord; the community is received into the Lord. He is the center, and from then on his grace and his demands constitute the whole Christian life. Although I live, no longer I live but he lives in me. Whoever sees me ought by rights to see the Lord in me. He ought to see, not that I have received the Lord, but that I am one who has been received by the Lord. He ought not even to notice that I have received the Lord, but ought always to see in me the one received by the Lord. That would correspond to the truth, and then I should have been assimilated to the truth.

Thus receiving the Lord is transmitted from the individual to the community. The personal consent we give the Lord dispossesses the individual in such a way that he belongs to Christ, who gives him to the community. Christ ought to live in the individual so that he lives in the community. There is indeed a personal relationship between the individual and the Lord, but no private relationship. The relationship is not in this respect a human one. If someone is invited by friends and they put their house at his disposal, he cannot go and drive them out of their rooms and take possession of them. But the Lord may dispose of our inward dwelling as he wishes. A guest could only do so out of selfishness; but the Lord may do so out of love. For the demands he makes are not made on his own account, but are made for the sake of God and his brethren. (And here one might add what the other Evangelists so often add: he gives back what he takes a hundredfold. A consideration that is rarely found in John's Gospel because it is only on the way to love, whereas love itself overlooks the fact.)

Man's consent is never wholehearted. It often conceals a great deal of selfishness. It is possible to receive the Lord for very egotistical reasons. For example, to ensure a quiet little niche in the beyond. But the moment the Lord takes our consent seriously and comes to us, he thrusts aside everything incompatible with his presence. Astounding though it may be, we can receive the Lord halfheartedly, and when he comes, he converts that half into a whole. We may start an action for selfish reasons, and the Lord in us makes it good and fruitful. For the halfhearted Yes we address to him is taken up into the perfect Yes he addresses to us—which is not an excuse for being lukewarm and taking things easy but a consolation to us all where others are concerned. What they have started not altogether well, the Lord will lead to a happy conclusion. For this reason, a man who is looking for the Lord halfheartedly need not at once be put in possession of a full and final explanation of all the demands and enlightened upon the real severity of Christianity. In due course, the Lord himself will expand that soul and make it capable of receiving more of him than it can receive at present.

To those who receive him he gives the *power to become children of God*. They become children of God because they receive him. For he is the Son of God, and by virtue of his life in us he not only has the power to be in us what he already is but also expressly allows us to participate in this power of his and in its possibilities. Through his presence in us, we become him in us: we become children of God. For through his presence, everything in us that is his becomes the property of the Father. We are unthinkable without that which he is in us; and out of that in us which is his, he makes a child of God. What that means can only gradually be realized; it is inchoate, a beginning, without limits and without end. We imagined that to be a child of God was something perfectly definite, a fact once and for all clearly established. A child grows till he reaches the stature of his parents, but the child of God grows on without noticing it. For what might the attainable stature of his Father be—of God? As we begin to be children of

God, the fact we had thought so clear and definite changes within us into eternal life, which is always in the beginning, with God, and overflows eternally.

The fact that we can become this inconceivable thing, this surpassing thing, is entirely dependent on God's power. But that is the very power he did not wish to reserve for himself alone, desiring to give us the power himself. Our part in this process is not a passive one, for after all he *lives* in us, and we live from his life. Our life becomes infinitely more active than it was before. It becomes active in an entirely new and unfamiliar sense. As long as we were only ourselves, we were really passive; we obeyed the law of the world, which orders us not to listen to the Lord. We were the playthings of a passion: not to listen to the Lord. Our soul was as if paralyzed. Now that we are become children of God, we move freely in the Lord and participate in his power over life. Once the Lord begins to live in us, we no longer have time for ourselves; our whole life becomes active because it is used for the Lord. We cannot simply "let him work in us" and observe how he lives in us. At each moment of our lives, we are called to the most intense, most vital participation.

When a man begins to believe and takes his first steps on the road of love, he begins by believing in the Name of the Lord. That is the beginning. It is not as yet love, not as yet unity in God, childhood, a mission. It is still belief in something particular, in the Bible as a fact, in the Church as a fact, in experience and education. For the moment, the Name covers everything he does not know, everything that has not yet become life. But believing in the Name, he has in his hands the Word to guide him forward and which, like a magic formula, opens all the doors. The Name gives him access to the mystery. This he *knows* even if at first he knows *that* and nothing else.

Even though he does not know the fullness of love. Even though he cannot really see what faith means. He simply feels that faith has entered into him and, with it, something that goes on growing greater and greater; he is conscious of the unknown growth that has no name. The Word that opens all doors is within him; suddenly he realizes that he has the highest power within him, even power over God. Power to compel God to recognize him as his son. The power that transforms the believer from a grateful recipient into one who makes demands. Who can come before the Father with the freedom of God's children to claim his rights and his inheritance. From then on, there are things that we can categorically demand of God. We can demand that of sinners he should make us children of God. We can demand that he should impart his Spirit to us. We can demand that we should be able to fulfill his will. We can demand that we should live in his Son. We can demand that everything should turn out for the best. We can demand eternal life. Of course we cannot ask for things that remain his to give: a vocation to the priesthood, this or that gift of grace within the Church. But we can ask for his love, and within that love he can withhold nothing.

This power over God does not merely grow parallel to the growth of faith. Many things may grow in those who begin to believe; various grafts in the soul, which aim somehow or other at God, may all grow and unfold; a man may learn from books, from others, from meditating, and learn a lot that is new about his faith, and experience will confirm him in his certainty. Together with all this there go a selfish hankering for inner quiet and calm and perhaps, too, a little bent toward love. All these things in the soul grow, unfold, are ennobled and purified. But beside them, behind them, throughout everything, there is something else growing, with no relation to anything else.

There is the growing perception that with all this one has power over God, which means that everything in us that is not yet love is irresistibly growing into love and even now obeys the law of love. It means that everything is converging on love from all quarters and that the point of love upon which all these lines converge is alive and active long before the lines have actually met. Everything somehow or other grows beyond itself and is unified by one demand: the demand for love. Power over God exists only in love, and that is why the soul to whom this power has been given is infallibly drawn into the Kingdom and the law of love. Everything in it, its whole life, is oriented as though by an unseen magnet. And the most varied components combine to produce one single effect.

This power is given to those who believe in the name of the Lord, given to them for their own. It springs, on the one hand, from the superfluity of love that comes from the Lord's Passion and from the Holy Spirit set free through the Cross; and, on the other hand, from the superfluity of love in the Mother of God's consent, which was infinitely open to God and solely at his service, so that God alone could, so to say, exploit it. This double superfluity is free. It covers our want. It converts our miserable beginning of faith and love, our wretched efforts, our hopeless failures, into power over God himself. And whoever receives that power knows that it is the work of the Lord's love and of his Mother's love. He knows that he was loved even as a sinner; but he also knows that the power is a real one, given to him as his own. Power coming from the Mother through the Son to the Father.

The content of this power is aimed at a single end: To them *he gave power to become children of God*. Their power lies in the fact of being children of God. God does not want to be alone when giving to his children; he wants to be moved by them to give them all. He wants to be overcome by us, as it were, defeated by us. The thought is ridiculous as long as we are what we are and present ourselves, as such, before God. But it is not ridiculous when we realize that the faith in us belongs to the Son, that the word of faith is part of the Word that was in the beginning with God and is deposited in God. It is no longer ridiculous when we know that everything was created through the Word, who is eternal life and shines in the darkness. And that this Word went out from God and irresistibly returns to God; that God recognizes the Word, when it comes to him, as his own. When we come to God with this Word, the Father recognizes it immediately, knows that it is his Word, and refuses it nothing. He sees in us, not the natural creature, but part of his Word. He recognizes the Son in us, and it is the Son in us that he loves and respects, and he cannot do otherwise than love us, because the Son is in us, and our presence is fortuitous. Because we happen to be the ones in whom the Son has placed his Word, which is life and light and power over God. It is not ridiculous, for it is the order that God himself ordained. We are what God expects. We are those whom God expects. He awaits the Son, the Son together with everything belonging to him and with the total effect of his love. The Son not only as the Head but as the Body, with his Church, with his whole creation. And since there is something of the Son in us, we must all return with him to the Father, for the Son cannot be separated from his mission, or his mission from its fulfillment. The Son made himself equal with his mission and with us. Part of that mission was to bring us back to his Father, who awaits us longingly because he awaits his Son.

This aspect of the Son's mission is the will of the Father, for the Son does nothing but the Father's will. That is why our victory over God, over the will of God, this power, which is given to us in faith, is the Father's will and nothing else.

Because we have the power, in faith, to overcome God, we ourselves are utterly overcome by his power. It all happens in such a way that it passes understanding. We ourselves understand nothing of what is happening or of what we are doing. Like a man bowled over by love, we are whirled by it into an abyss, into the abyss of childhood in God, where, altogether inconceivably, we are treated as though we were one with the Son of God. It is so far beyond our comprehension that, instead of accepting it as a condition in which to remain and rest, we are as if startled into asking ourselves who we really are. We have risen from recognizing the Son to faith in the Son, and from that to unity in love and in sonship. But that unity cannot be held fast. We step back into faith and finally stand before the Son, who is alone worthy in the eyes of God, whereas we are unworthy. The path from the Son to unity is not a path on which we grow but a path on which we grow less before the Son. The way of faith does not allow us to regard being the children of God as the end of our wanderings; it is a path whose only law is the service of God and of his Son; it is a way that is a mission. The thought of being children of God and demanding to be such is one that demands more faith and more love, which are immediately placed at the service of the Son's mission. We must decrease, not through love of self-effacement or with the aim of obliterating ourselves, but for love's sake and on account of the Lord's prodigality, in which we now have an active part.

On the road of faith, from the Son to the Father, we are like people who have amassed vast fortunes, but, being a treasure of love, it is so immeasurably great that we cannot grasp it or keep it; indeed, the fortune we possess is of such a kind that it must be distributed again. Once the love of God flows over us who have become his children, we realize that it wants nothing for itself—it consists solely in giving. We join in the prodigality of the Lord and are prodigal of ourselves. To whom? To all those who have not yet received the light. And also to all those who have, in fact, received it but whose need is not satisfied—whether they are still on the way to becoming the children of God or whether subjectively they have not recognized and understood the nature of the gift they received with the grace of childhood in God. For many are bathed in grace without knowing it: children of God whose eyes are closed. And, finally, to all those who are prodigal of themselves, and perhaps there is no deeper form of community than the community of those who are dedicated in the Son.

The way of faith from the Son to the Father, and from the Father to the Son, is trinitarian. The Son is born in us through the Father, and he unfolds his life in us through the Holy Spirit, and we return with the Son, in the Spirit, to the Father, but only to be sent out again in eternity with the Son, in the Spirit. On the way from the Son to the Father, the Son transforms us, and the Father receives us as his children; and on the way from the Father to the Son, the Father perfects our childhood by allowing us to participate in the Son's mission. The mission with which we are sent out is an echo of the Son's trinitarian mission. Once the trinitarian life begins to unfold in us and we have become children of God, once the Trinity comes into our souls and the three Persons have lovingly become one in us, we are sent out on the trinitarian mission.

The unity of our life and of our mission is a unity of love and therefore a trinitarian unity. It is a matter of total indifference how the mission is then formed in the individual; it can be as imperceptible, as hidden, as contemptible as you please. Its trinitarian sense may be completely concealed. It is not, for that reason, less strong or vital and is carried out with the same strength as the Son's mission is carried out in us. Neither the one who dispenses love nor the one who receives it need perceive its trinitarian essence. Perhaps both of them feel only dimly that the work is accomplished in love. The power of this love is hidden, but it is the same infinite power that was given to us to become children of God. On the road from the Son to the Father, the Son gave us power over the Father. On the road from the Father to the Son, the Father gives us, as his children, the power that he gave the Son over the men within our mission.

The power in question is part of the life principle of Christianity, the vitality that gives it its drive even in the eyes of the disinterested spectator. This power is a looking-glass reflection, a pendant, a counterweight to the powerlessness of the Lord on the Cross—he himself dying and powerless, the Church herself scattered and everything seemingly in dissolution. And, in contrast, the enormous power given to the individual Christian, the power that is placed in his hands, the fruit of the overflowing love of the Son dying powerless. This astonishing power is born of his weakness, born at all times into the whole world. The power that he gave me, the last among sinners, of being able to do what I will with God—what he has given me to will. And, moreover, power is given to me, not over a weak, but over an all-powerful God, a strong and mighty God. It is not as if the superfluity of love that is given me were powerful because God himself had become weak, or as if God were moved by the weakness of his Son and overcome by it, or as if God succumbed to the strength and power of youth like an emotional old man. It is not as if God had allowed himself to be carried away by enthusiasm for his Son, or in the excess of his suffering had granted everything if only he might no longer hear of that suffering. On the contrary, the power to become children of God strikes upon a God in the fullness of his power. It is love in the fullness of health, expressing itself in its inconceivable contrary: the Lord on the Cross, dying and weak, and we, living in the power to become children of God.

THE MAN BORN OF GOD

1:13. *Who are born, not of blood nor of the will of the flesh nor of the will of man, but of God.*

Not of blood means without regard to sex, race, family ties, kith or kin, tradition, inheritance, without regard to all the limitations that are the fruit of procreation and birth. *The will of the flesh* means the will of instinct and impulse; *the will of man* is the will of spiritual man, who looks for devotion, not satisfaction, in love. One can beget a child from pure instinct; one can also beget children who are the fruit of the complete man, body and spirit, ordered within marriage. But though the child of a properly ordered marriage is other than the child of pleasure, marriage can never produce a child of God. The child of God can only be *born of God*.

To be born of God is a mystery. No man has seen God. No one was present when he begot his Son; no one witnessed the creation, nor can anyone witness the birth of a man born of God. God gives birth in secret. Nor are we told that the children of God are born of the Father, but of God. Formerly the power to become children of God seemed to resemble our capacity to enter the life of the Trinity and to learn the way from the Son to the Father and from the Father to the Son in the Spirit. One had imagined the life of God as flowing on eternally and harmoniously, a great arc of love, a clear, orderly exchange of love. But now, when a man is born of God, there is nothing left but the excess and the superfluity, which appear to us as disorder—the pure and shattering absolute. For a man born of God is thrust forth from God. He is expelled and flung out of the security in God in which he had hitherto cradled himself. Everything happens as though the hand of God, which had hitherto led him gently along, had suddenly become a high-tension cable. And as he receives the life of God, he sinks unconscious to the ground, robbed of his spirit.

No man has seen God. He is accessible to us in the Son, through faith, love, and hope, through the life of the sacraments. God lives for us in the gifts he has given us. As long as these gifts of his are given to us, we can grasp them; we can also have some intimation of the distinction of the Persons in God. But the Word returns to God. Faith, love, and hope and the sacraments return to God. For everything was in the beginning with God and remains with God and returns to God: the Word itself is God, and when God becomes all in all, faith, love, and hope and the sacraments are ultimately God. God is faith because he is the answer; God is hope because he is the consolation; God is love because he is the fulfillment. He is all this to us in the sacraments, which pour forth grace and exhaust themselves in love. But when everything is resolved into love, it enters the mystery of explosive unity. Prior to love, everything is disjointed and cannot become one. If there were no sin, faith would resolve itself into love. Everything that is whole and entire is love pure and simple. Those who are born of God are touched by the surpassing mystery of the unity of love—infinitely above distinctions and beyond notions.

The birth is accomplished in such absolute secrecy that to the majority of men it remains completely hidden. They have grace without knowing how they received it. They are children of God without knowing what it means. They live in faith, love, and hope as the gift of God, and they also receive the sacraments, baptism above all, as a gift of God, but they fail to realize the extent to which these gifts sustain them in returning to God. In that we can discern something of the forbearance of God, something of the original grace given to Adam. Adam was born of God in the sleep of creation, and Eve was born of God in the sleep of Adam's creation. Their birth was already behind them when they awoke to existence; it raised no problem. Chaos no longer prevailed, and men had not yet produced a new chaos by distinguishing between good and evil. They lived without questioning anything and lived in God, and God himself bridged the distance to them through grace, so that he might not be the occasion of shattering them by his presence. But when the chaos of sin opened, and man became conscious of that chaos, God—of his grace—punished man by making him give birth in pain; and to be born of God in grace became infinitely more painful. For it is man in chaos—conscious of his own chaos—who has now to be born of God, reborn out of the order and the glory of God, which, compared with this chaos, appear as the absolute opposite: the inconceivable.

The external convulsions that followed on the Son's birth—the expulsion from Nazareth, from Bethlehem, and finally from Judea, the poverty, the uncertainty—these external convulsions are distant symbols that enable us to perceive something of the inner convulsion that followed when the eternally begotten of God was born of God here and now, into our sinful flesh, in chaos and in darkness. Those close to him are all increasingly shaken by the convulsion: his Mother, in fear before the angel, trembles before the Holy Spirit, a fear and trembling that grow throughout her life until she expires with her crucified Son and finally ascends with him as the apocalyptic woman. At first the apostles are spared this fear and trembling, but they too experience something of the explosive and shattering nature of birth from God in the fire of the Passion; and so that the faith of the Church should remain vital, Paul, on the road to Damascus, experienced the lightning of new birth more profoundly than the Twelve—and was left from that time to consume himself in zeal for God. All important missions in the Church start with such a birth, because those with a significant mission have things to communicate that can be learned only from that kind of shattering shock.

But even they will never know the moment of birth, for it is hidden in the inmost mystery of God, but only the moment after when, as men born of God, as newborn men, they feel the power of the new life in their limbs. They are not sensible of an illumination or of anything touching their selves; they will feel nothing pleasing, no foreboding of great things, only a sort of chaos without distinction or form; they will be without the capacity to discern or understand or to see the way. The newborn man is like someone who has survived a catastrophe, a man just saved, a survivor who opens his eyes again and hardly recognizes the things about him. He has the feeling of having in some inconceivable way been transplanted; nothing is any longer the same, least of all himself. What has happened is the opposite of an organic growth; it is a sudden transition into a new state of being. The man born of God has first of all to accustom himself to this new state. He does not in the first instance call upon God. Nor does he call for sight, vision, perspective, and a standard. He merely feels the immeasurable violence of the impact, and his only desire is to collect himself. He sees himself lying there with all his limbs intact but needs to make sure it is the same person; he knows that he is saved but no longer knows who he is. He is a man whom God has overwhelmed. Touched by the life that was in the beginning with God, he was flung to the ground. He is a child of God, but without knowing what that means.

A man may have lived for years in a state of grace when all of a sudden the lightning strikes at the very center of his Christian life. It is not necessarily the beginning of the life of God in him. The beginning may have been gentle, hardly perceptible, until suddenly the great earthquake occurs and shatters his life to pieces. But once a man has trembled at the shock, he is marked for life. Something in him is awakened that alters everything, in the same way that a young man's uneventful home life is suddenly overturned by a burning passion for a woman. Everything in him is uprooted and exposed to the light, and he realizes that he has never known what the love of God means. He sees something that he can never forget but that others do not see, and he will never again know rest. He has emerged from surroundings into which he can never fit again.

That does not mean that he is a better Christian than others or even a better man morally speaking. The reverse may well be true. The shock of the earthquake may have unfitted him altogether for ordinary, regular work, filling his soul with unrest. A man who knows nothing of all this may do his duty more conscientiously. Perhaps he says his prayers more regularly and performs more good works; his judgment may be balanced and calmer, and his work marked by greater prudence, more self-control. He will be able, without danger, to test his own humility and love of God, to examine his conscience and consider his actions and learn to improve himself. But if there is one thing that is forbidden the man born of God, it is precisely that—to measure himself against his achievement. Nothing, he finds, is so unbearable as the sight of what he has achieved. He is consumed in a sort of despair by the thought of all that has not been done. He can see only the distance that separates him from God, the total lack of correspondence. And his whole existence is concentrated in a single passion, imparted by that unbearable dissonance. Others may genuinely regard themselves as useless servants, while resting in faith and love. They will try most earnestly to improve themselves out of love for God. But the man of whom we are speaking looks upon his work as straw, fit only for the fire. His faith takes the form of impossibility, his love the form of unattainability. But the fire of the impossible is his very life, and it makes him creative. This does not mean to say that everything will work out well and that all the consequences of his experience are willed by God. The gulf between feeling and doing is perhaps all too great. Men who have been buried alive or barely escaped from a burning house bear the wound permanently in their soul. For the rest of their lives, they bear the stigma of the catastrophe. Forever after they are left trembling, and that may often be a hindrance for much that is good.

The man born of God is like a man distraught. What he hears about God never corresponds to what he knows of God. All his thoughts about God are inadequate compared with what God revealed to him, and he is driven to despair. He can no longer bear to look at himself. He lives on the fact that God is ever greater. As he awakens from the shock that struck him and begins to take his bearings (though he will never again be certain of them), he can see things only from God's point of view. Having experienced God as "ever greater", the world inevitably seems "ever smaller". To all appearances he is wearing blinkers where the values of the world are concerned. His outlook seems narrowed. The way to God has been widened by God himself till it includes absolutely everything. Where he is concerned, the equilibrium between God and the world is destroyed forever.

He has not forgotten his former state. Moreover, he sees it incorporated in the men about him. The first life, too, may have been beautiful, and its beauty is not forgotten; but it is a beauty that lies far below him now, because it is incompatible with the surpassing beauty of the new life. The newborn man lives between heaven and earth and cannot settle down in either. Not on earth, because he has been transplanted into heaven; not in heaven, because he has to live as one expelled from the inconceivable God. And the fact that he is no longer of the world reveals the power of the new birth to him: he, who had been worldly, so rooted in this world, was uprooted forever by that power. His previous state forms a sort of background that throws his present state into relief and reveals the whole change and all that no longer matters.

The shock of being born of God has nothing to do with the religious agitation produced by the contemplation of nature. One may be moved to tears and stirred to one's depths at the sight of created beauty, and the feeling may be accompanied by a devout lifting of the spirit to God. But the shock of natural beauty never merges into the shock of being reborn. Nature affords no parallel and still less any starting point.

From a worldly point of view, the man born of God is a plant that has had its stem bent double. Before the injury, it flourished as a wonderful system of veins in which the sap rose and fell; its healthy closed system was a harmonious life capable of unfolding in suitable surroundings. And suddenly its stem is bent double by a strange hand. Only that death is no way out; it has got to adapt itself as best it can and go on living. He is like a man who has had an operation that entirely changes his metabolism: he has got to go on living as best he can under new conditions, just as if nothing had happened. And in fact, from then on, his whole life assumes a new character; he lives "as if".

As long as man has not experienced the explosion of being reborn, it is easy for him to live as a member of the community. Afterward, it becomes difficult. It may be that the new life leads to absolute solitude in God, although love for others persists and perhaps even grows greater. The approach to men is made difficult; language is no longer quite the same. It may even be that a man thus touched by God has not got the human strength needed to bear the shock, and his spirit may be darkened. The experience of God's surpassing greatness is beyond his powers, and he breaks under the strain. Or it may be that one who has seen what God is demands too much of others and becomes an unbearable member of the community. He is no longer available for harmless, light, and easy conversation. He may be incapable of constructive work within the established order. He is withdrawn from men and no longer understood by them. He is so overwhelmed and shattered by God that he is not much good for ordinary undertakings.

But his isolation is not a form of pride, nor does it resemble the isolation that springs from dread of life or some other pathological cause, even when that isolation is draped in a religious mantle, as it very often is. The man born of God is isolated by God himself. It may well be that the community grasps something of what is happening and can select something fruitful from the rim of the explosion. But the community never penetrates to the center of the vortex, which is a secret between the individual and God. And yet that secret is a secret of love and so of fruitfulness.

The shards that remain after an earthquake are fragments of love and so of unity. They are witnesses to the act of fecundation whose explosive effect scatters a superfluity of power.

Seen from inside, such men are a source of life; seen from outside, they are a sign from God. They are a sign that one cannot keep in step with God. A sign that breaks through the stream of the Church's Tradition. The man born of God is flung out of the usual channels and, consequently, out of the Church's Tradition. And it is part of the Church's Tradition that from time to time men will be thus thrown out. The Kingdom of God does not, after all, grow out of the ground like a plant. It is not only organic; it is always apocalyptic. Every catastrophe in which God appears is a center of fruitfulness. Every explosion that originates in God increases the power of the Church. Inroads like that nourish it for generations. It is not the man blown sky high who is nourished—how should he be?—but the place he occupied, where he vanished into God, opens the way for a sight of God. God reveals himself through the opening created, and generations of men live on that revelation. The place where it happens may become a place of pilgrimage, though it is not the place that matters but *what* happened; and those who go to the shrine should be moved, not by the place, but by God, who, on that very spot, once set everything aside and appeared to man. At first the Church regards a catastrophe of this order as a misfortune until she has learned through the blessings it brings that God has revealed himself. Until she gradually comes to see that her forms retain their vitality and life only if her Tradition and framework are from time to time burst open.

THE WORD MADE FLESH

1:14a. *And the Word became flesh and dwelt among us.*

The children of God are not born of the flesh; they are born of God alone. But they would not have been born of God had the Word not become flesh, had the Son not taken our substance, and the Spirit not taken flesh. The spiritual Word became flesh so that our flesh might become spiritual. Because the Son became as we are, we can become as he is: children of God.

The Incarnation should not be considered in the light of the Virgin Birth so much as in the light of the fact that, like us, the Lord had an earthly Mother, a Mother of flesh and blood who nourished him from her body and fed him with her milk. That he did not live above us but among us, on the same level of the flesh as we do. As a body among other bodies, a man among men. He himself was the Word, and he remained the Word. He communicated himself to us in the flesh because he was flesh like us, and spiritually because he was the Word, which was in the beginning with God. Being flesh and spirit simultaneously, he reaches our spirit through our bodies and spiritually soaks our bodies through and through, so that what is spirit in us and what is his spirit in us may return to the Father. If he had not lived among us, our bodies would have returned to dust. And what would have become of our spirit? Everything would fail and fall, both body and spirit. But as it is, everything will rise again; the body participates in the Resurrection because the Son has a body; the spirit participates because it is in communion with the Spirit of the Lord.

His faith in us was that we would recognize him and believe in his flesh. He showed us his love by coming from the Father to the flesh, and we in our turn must show him our love by going from the flesh to the Father. His hope was to become flesh in order that it might be our hope to become spirit. Because we were mere flesh before his coming, we could grasp the union of the Son and the Father only in the separation of the Son from the Father in the flesh. We should never have understood what the Son in God meant had we not seen him with our own eyes in the flesh.

The Word became flesh: body and spirit can therefore never be separated in faith, love, and hope, that is to say, in the Catholic Church. The whole sphere of body and spirit is open to Catholic man, and neither of them is forgotten. There is, on the one hand, the balanced harmony between the two whereby the center of gravity in a life, in a marriage, may at one time, and during a particular phase of life, be more in the spirit or more in the flesh. Both are in order within the framework of the subordination of the flesh to the spirit. And then too, since the Word was spiritual in its Incarnation, and since we must reach the Father through the incarnate Word, there is also the possibility that in the place of this balanced harmony—marriage—the center of gravity may be entirely transposed into the spirit. Then the flesh may be absorbed into the spirit and almost forgotten, or it may be utterly separated from the spirit and borne as a burden on earth, a penance, a thorn that we must bear with us—and the rebellion of the impulses and the struggle with them lasts a lifetime. The whole breadth of these possibilities is embraced in the fact that the Lord was in the flesh and that he was so in pure love. The surpassing love of the Lord is the criterion of every possible relation between the spirit and the flesh. That is to say, his love is the norm of the relation between the spirit and the flesh in every particular instance, however different or even opposed they may be. And because the Lord was in the flesh, we need no longer love ourselves in the flesh but can love the Lord in the flesh. And because he lived in our spirit through the flesh, we need not love ourselves in the spirit but can serve him in the spirit.

The Word became flesh means, further, that contemplation becomes action. The Word that comes from the Father comes from contemplation. The Son in the Father is contemplation, comes down upon earth to action, and returns to contemplation. But if he was pure contemplation before his birth, then his whole earthly life was both contemplation and action. The thirty years in Nazareth were primarily contemplative; the three years of work were primarily active. But even being active, he never ceased to be contemplative. And when he returns into the contemplation of the Father, he bears his action with him: his contemplation is different and richer than it was formerly. Since the Incarnation, there are only shades of difference in the inseparable unity of action and contemplation; in the most active moments, he was contemplative; in the most contemplative, active.

The Word became flesh means, furthermore, that the Word proclaimed must become act of charity. When the Word thus becomes act, charity in the end becomes Word again. For each time God sends forth the Word, it bears with it the movement of return to God. Charity here is to be understood simply as a concrete act of love, the giving of alms, for example (alms that may be collected after the word of the sermon); and as everything done for the poor, the sick, the dying, for prisoners. Through these seemingly corporal works of mercy, the poor return to the spirit: care for the body, because the Word was made flesh, becomes communication of the spiritual Word, and so the Word comes alive for those who do not possess it. The act of giving that occurs in giving alms is not exhausted in the gift; even if it is given without a word, it goes on to the Word of God and leads back to him.

The Word became flesh means, finally, that Christian parents in their sacramental marriage not only beget the body and flesh of their child. The child of Christian parents is also born and begotten of the spirit, of the sacramental word of their marriage. So that even before he is baptized, he is a different child from the child of pagan parents. He is born of the spirit because he springs from a sacrament. The spirit of marriage becomes flesh, which in its turn becomes spirit, for example, through the baptism of the child. And then again, in a wider sense, through extreme unction and a Christian death. For it is the parents' sacramental marriage that prepares the way for extreme unction, which is, in a sense, contained in the effect of that grace. There is a relationship between the two sacraments, a common origin.

The daily inclusion of the incarnate Word in our lives is the Our Father. It starts with an invocation of the Father. It goes on to beg for the flesh and returns to the spirit in the prayer for salvation. The bread we pray for is, in the first place, our earthly bread, but it is also the eucharistic Bread, the Word made flesh. The Eucharist is the perpetual reminder of the Incarnation in our lives, the Our Father its daily inclusion.

The Word made flesh *dwelt among us*. That means it is not a theory, a myth, a philosophy, a religious system, but quite simply the presence of the Lord among us. God lived the life of a man among us; he brought before our eyes and gave a visible demonstration of what it means to live for God on earth. He did so within limits that are ours and within possibilities accessible to all of us. Everything in his life can be verified, every detail tested experimentally; everything is on the level on which we live. He is like the son of a rich employer who offers to live with the poorest of his father's workers in order to test whether one can really manage on the wages and in those conditions. He deposits his entire inheritance with his Father, so that on the Cross he will no longer know that he possesses it—he surrenders his divinity; and he takes for the road no more than we have, through his grace: faith, love, and hope; he lives among us in the identical conditions in which we live. And proves that it can be done: that one can live a perfect Christian life in this world in spite of darkness and death. He shows us that, within the closed frontiers of this existence of ours, one can lead a life that is entirely open toward God, entirely dependent upon God. He receives everything from God: from the Father and from himself as the Son. He receives it in the unity of both and shows us that to be a Christian also means to expect and to receive everything in the unity of Father and Son. He receives his whole life as a gift from the Trinity; his inmost attitude is confidence, the unity of faith, love, and hope that lives entirely in God, of God, and for God. He knows that the moment will come when even the gifts of faith, love, and hope will have to be surrendered and deposited with God and that the Father alone will dispose of them. He himself will be in darkness, but he is reconciled to that. He lives our earthly life in time altogether in the Father. In doing so, he is the perfect Christian. And as such he dwelt among us.

1:14b. ... *Full of grace and truth. We have beheld his glory, glory as of the only-begotten Son from the Father.*

We have seen the Spirit in the flesh. We have seen the invisible in the visible. We have seen the Father in the Son. We have seen the immediate mediated in the Mediator. We have seen the grace that is God's eternal truth in the truth into which his grace transplants us.

The difference between truth and grace resembles the difference between life and light. Grace comes solely from God; it is something to which we can never compare ourselves, something we can only receive and that never becomes our own property, that we can transmit but never possess as our substance. Grace is always with God, even though *we* transmit it, so that, in spite of us, it is he who transmits it. We never communicate it as we communicate our knowledge or a truth we have understood.

Truth, in contrast, belongs to us as well as to God. We cannot refuse the grace of God, but we can refuse God. We can refuse to put ourselves in the state in which we can receive grace, the state in which grace becomes truth for us. Naked grace before naked man cannot be refused. When a man is inundated with grace, the giver is God alone; man is not consulted. In contrast, God's truth becomes truth for us only when we stand ready for it, when we say Yes to it. Truth is not only knowledge but also effect. That God is great may be true for him; it is true for us only when we recognize its truth and allow it to work in us and move us. For us, divine truth is a result produced. Were it to remain in the stage of mere theoretical correctness, God's truth could be apprehended by reason alone, and the propositions could be divided and classified even before they had been received as a whole. When God says, I am great, then it is true because he says it. But man knows this truth only when he has acknowledged it, and that is why one part of truth is with God and one part with man.

Full of grace means: there is such a fullness of grace that it cannot be subdivided. *Full of truth*, in contrast, includes the division already mentioned, one part being with God, the other with man. One part of my knowledge that God is great is with God, because he has said it. The other part lies in the fact that he convinces me of his greatness through his utterance. This effect lies contained in his Word, because God at once expects me to act accordingly, so that he can act in me. God alone works in grace. In truth, on the contrary, there is decision. Where truth is concerned, man must answer. The concept of truth, therefore, belongs to the concept of faith. When grace appears, its appearance is comparable to a natural phenomenon. Truth, however, presupposes that man thinks and answers, that he has the capacity for decision in God. Grace is an absolute that shines from God. In truth, man is the relative, drawn into God's radiance. In the truth, he receives grace and catches sight of grace, which is the glory of God. For the *glory of God that we have beheld* is the glory of his grace. There is a movement between grace and truth, and they circulate, as it were, one within the other: grace goes out from God, and its effect in us is that we receive it as the truth. The truth received opens our eyes to the essence of grace, leads us to the light of contemplation in which we catch sight of the glory of grace.

The glory of grace is not the absolute glory of God but *the glory as of the only-begotten Son from the Father.* Those who are born of God and have become inwardly aware of the mystery of supreme and living unity are touched by the supreme mystery of the glory of God. The glory of his unity is such that it cannot do otherwise than communicate itself: the movement that circulates from God and back to God in faith, love, and hope, in the mission and the sacraments, is not a movement from unity to plurality and back to unity but contains the original, unity itself, and as such contains the Word. The supreme mystery is that this unity is to such a degree one and unique that it must express itself and sends forth the Son. That God can give no stronger proof of this unity, which is his glory, than beget the Son. The glory of the Father in his unity is so great that he cannot do otherwise than give his glory to God himself, that is, to the Son. The Father therefore demonstrates his glory and his unity by giving his Son to the world and communicates himself to us in the Son, for in no other way can he communicate the uniqueness of his unity. Having no one to whom he can give his glory, he must give it to all by sending forth the Son. If the Father's solitude and glory were only relative, he would have to make himself a way to man, to each individual man; he would have to bridge the gulf, as it were. But being in absolute solitude, he has the Son in him, who is the revelation and the way and the gate. To be two is ultimately supreme solitude, so that to express his perfect glory, God needs only to point toward the Son, who comes from the Father and is so unique that he has everything from the Father.

True solitude and true love are one. If a man desires a son, he must lose something of his substance; he must give it to be born of a woman. In order to be two, he must be in solitude. God gives his substance in giving his Son to the world, but he is always two in order to be alone. The parallel is therefore at the same time a contrast. Correspondingly, woman, in order to be alone—as in the time of her pregnancy, though the period of motherhood is also solitude—woman must receive the seed from outside. She receives what is foreign to her from man and receives the other substance, which she lets ripen in solitude. Then she must surrender the foreign being so as to be two again. What she receives in order to be alone is foreign; what she gives back in order to return to joint life is her own. The same thing occurs in the community: in order to belong to the Church, I must surrender myself, and then I am no longer alone but a member. But before I can do so, I must receive what is foreign from the Church in order to be alone and give it back as my own to the Church in order to lead a communal life. Each member of the Church must surrender himself in order that others may receive grace. For in the Church, the solitude of each and every one is the perfection of the community, and when each has surrendered himself and exists only in devotion to his neighbor, thus becoming absolutely alone—alone because abandoned, surrendered, and still more alone because he has received his neighbor in place of himself—then comes God with his grace, takes over the solitude of each individual, and makes it fruitful. That grace is the grace of contemplation, which is always solitary and in which we have seen his glory.

And, finally, the glory we have spoken about is the Host, which we see with our own eyes. For the only Son is so unique that he is in truth everywhere, in millions of separate Hosts, which demonstrate their unity in numbers that cannot be reckoned. There is no other medium through which to demonstrate the uniqueness of the glory except infinite dissemination. The number that cannot be reckoned is complete, however, only when each one of us receives the Host. When the Son has communicated himself so that each one of us participates in God, unity in the Lord is once more established. The unity of the Lord is reached when the dissemination of the Lord is complete. A stone can occupy a definite space only when it has been completely pulverized; then the dust hangs in the air and fills the whole space evenly. When the dispersal is complete, Christ can be recognized immediately. When the Host reaches every man, it need no longer remain Host but becomes the one and only Christ, who need no longer distribute his Real Presence. For then distance ceases to be; there is no such thing as remoteness, there is only proximity, and symbols become superfluous.

1:15. *John bore witness to him, and cried, This was he of whom I said, He who comes after me ranks before me, for he was before me.*

For he was from eternity in the Father. He is the Word in the beginning. He is the fulfillment, and because he is the Word, he is also the promise. And being the fulfillment of his own promise, he is the one who comes after, without coming late. Because he is the Alpha, he is also the Omega.

Time must be considered not only as flowing out from God but also as flowing back into God, for beginning and end are one. The clouds produce rain, but rain also produces clouds. And what is true of time is equally true of place and, ultimately, of all words expressing a relation: whence, through what, whither, since when. The answer to every question in the world lies hidden in the Father. There is no question that was not first of all an answer. All questions come from the answer and return to the answer. The answer is with the Father, and the Father has allowed us all the questions he allowed the Son, both because he fears none and because his children have the right to ask them. Each one of our questions is answered, though many of us fail to hear the answer because we are not in the proper state to understand it. I can ask God what I like;

and, having given me the power to ask, he bound himself to answer. But those who do not hear it can always explain the answer as wanting or misunderstand it as nonexistent. Silence, too, is an answer. And God's answer sometimes sounds very different from the one we expect; in itself it is adequate, but man is not. And so we search for an explanation, when we are simply not in that state of immediateness that gives us direct access to the answer. Sin hampers our understanding.

1:16. *And from his fulness have we all received, grace upon grace.*

The fullness is both, equally: both the one and indivisible, which cannot be analyzed or broken up into faith, love, and hope, and that which is thus broken up and differentiated in missions, offices, and tasks and dispensed in the grace of the sacraments. But the particularized always contains the undifferentiated. The whole unity is alive in each individualized part. When we receive the grace of baptism, we receive, not a partial grace, but grace whole and entire. We receive baptism fulfilled, baptism as the fullness. Not only the fullness of faith, love, and hope, but fullness as such. Fullness is the unity of all particularity. It is achieved, not by the obliteration of differences, but through their maximum enhancement in love. Though God created us as individuals, that individualization is nothing compared with the individualization imposed upon us when we are baptized into the unity.

God individualized us and marked us as men coming from him, from the Alpha. In baptism, he signs us as men returning to him, to the Omega—a far deeper mark. When a shepherd marks his flock, he stamps them with a sign that marks them his. But he cannot mark them so that they will return to him. Of course, if someone finds a strayed sheep and brings it back to him, it does return. But the cause of its return is external. When God marks a man, his stamp, sign, and impress are more than a mere mark of origin, though the fulfillment of the sign lies with man. In baptism, God gives him the freedom to return to him. Many people misunderstand this freedom and regard it as compulsion. They imagine that man, marked as God's creature, can reach his certain home in God freely, whereas baptism, they suppose, is a form of compulsion used by God to force us to return to him. Yet it is that "compulsion" that gives us the widest possible freedom, and through it the balance between "must" and "ought" is perfectly maintained; nothing is more necessary in love than freedom.

Grace upon grace. God gives me the grace of baptism, and I give him the grace of my return to him. He gives me the grace of allowing me to ask him anything, and I give him the grace of perhaps understanding the answer. He gives me the grace of sending me out, and I give him the grace of acting as his representative. And finally, by virtue of his grace, he gives me the human grace to meet sin, to recognize it in the light of his grace, to overcome it with the help of his grace, and to allow it to be extinguished in me through his grace; and I give him the grace of receiving his absolution. For although all grace comes from God, although it comes from him personally and is given to me, the receiver, personally, nevertheless the relation of God to man in grace is such that he desires my grace and gratitude. And there is a point of equilibrium between the grace of God and man's gratitude where God no longer considers the ultimate origin of grace. For what God gives he gives absolutely and entirely, giving us the right of ownership, even though everything ultimately comes from him. As one baptized, I am of course baptized through the grace of God, yet in the eyes of God I really own that grace. And in order to receive his grace back from me as though it were mine, he regards his Son's grace as an image and model of independent grace. The Son is God, but he too is God through God, and his grace is grace through God. And sending out his Son, with his own grace, the grace that was given to him, he created a sort of precedent. He allowed the Son to give us his grace so generously in the redemption that he no longer distinguishes in the fullness of that grace between the Son's grace and ours.

1:17. *For the law was given through Moses; grace and truth came through Jesus Christ.*

The use of *for* at this point means that the law is contrasted with the grace and truth that came through Jesus Christ and with the fullness that we have all received. The law is neither the fullness, nor have all received it, nor does it contain grace and truth. The law is only a preparation, a preliminary stage, hardly more than the scaffolding for the house to be built. Once the house is standing, the scaffolding is superfluous. With the appearance of grace and truth, that is to say, the love of Christ, we leave the law behind us. For although the law is good and comes from God, it is related to sin. And as the Lord's grace wipes out sin, it leaves the law behind and renders it obsolete.

The law is related to sin if only because it forbids it without offering man the strength to avoid it. More dangerous still, the very existence of the law is a temptation to man to measure his actions by its rule. And with the law for his rule, he must try to be just. When a man who

tries to keep the law humbly recognizes that he has trans-
gressed such and such a law so and so many times, the
background of his transgressions is the tacit but nonetheless
clear implication that he has kept it in other respects. His
transgressions stand out in relief against the background of
his observance. A Christian who confesses that he has not
been to Mass on three Sundays implies that he has fulfilled
his duty at other times. Anyone who measures his life by
the law has a standard in his hand.

The law binds a man to himself and hinders him from
binding himself to God. The law is always finite and limited: one can work one's way to the end of it. That is
why it does not free our gaze for God, who is unending
and unbounded, our relation to whom is without end.
Man can in fact try to observe the law. He can make a
speciality of it, do the daily exercises, and even break all
records. But what has that to do with God? Absorbed in
his exercises, he is utterly absorbed in himself and has no
time for God. The law creates a third class of men half-
way between ordinary sinners, who simply know they
have sinned, and those who are redeemed in the love of
Christ. It consists of those who can justify themselves.
Of those who sometimes succeed in clambering up the
ladder of perfection that their reason has elaborated and
their will has set as aim. It consists of those who reach
the end they have set themselves or, if they don't attain
it at once, at any rate never lose courage or give up hope
of reaching it one day. At least they hope to approach
the ideal. They plan to master their sins and mistakes, to
cultivate and practice their virtues, and see to it that their
virtues outweigh their sins. It is not an impossible task,
for they have in their hands a standard of good and evil.
And it is quite possible, or at least not impossible, for
them to accomplish what is prescribed.

The good set before them in the law is a definite sum; it consists of a definite amount, and given time and patience one can gradually add part to part and complete the total. It may be necessary at one period in life to see things in this light. On the threshold of manhood, morality reveals its meaning, and a young man will come to understand what it means to do good and avoid evil. An idealist will probably take it as his aim, and, by doing good and particularly by not doing evil, he may hope in time to become perfect. But in pursuing his course, he will inevitably reach the crossroads where everything is decided. Either he will keep the yardstick in his own hands and become a pharisee, or he will step beyond the standpoint of the law, sink his good and his evil in the grace and truth of Christ, and leave the yardstick in the hands of God. Then he will realize that fullness is not found in the law and that the law, being finite, simply cannot communicate fullness. He will understand that the one love of the New Covenant implies a far greater obligation than all the laws of the Old Covenant put together. For love knows no limits; it is infinite in the proper sense; it means eternal growth and increase. It puts an end to all our calculations.

It is only in the infinity of love that man experiences what the good is in truth. And that is why it is only then that he discovers what evil, what sin is in truth. Those who know what love means know that in confessing their sins on the basis of the law, they are unable to speak of their real sins. The law is simply incapable of registering or expressing their sins. Even if a man has really committed the various wrongs that he confesses, the sum of these formulated wrongs is never identical with his sin before God. An accusation formulated according to the law is a symbolic accusation. But when a sinner who knows what love is examines his conscience in order to show it to God in confession, he sees within his soul a formless swamp of sin, with all sorts of half-submerged objects projecting from it. He catches hold of a few, of as many as he can hold, so as to give the swamp some sort of form. But he knows perfectly well that he is not exhausting the swamp; behind the contour he has given his sins lies the formless and immense pool of his sinfulness. All that remains unsaid, that he will never be able to say. All that he has forgotten, that he never fully knew, that he will never be able to see. In the moment of absolution, he feels the boundlessness of the unsaid: the greatness of the grace that pours in upon him enables him to gauge the greatness of the guilt forgiven him. How deep the vessel must be that needs so much to fill it!

The grace and truth of Christ mark the end of the grace and truth of the law; finite grace and truth are surpassed by infinite grace and truth.

There was *grace*, too, in the Old Covenant, but grace that was still entirely in God and with God, in suspension, as it were, above the world, beyond man's reach. On God's side was infinity; on man's side, all was still finite. God's grace lay in giving man a law that corresponded to his limitations. Within the framework of this finite norm, man could attain a limited perfection. But measured by the infinite standard of God, the finite framework fell to pieces. That is why God sent his Son into the world: so as not to measure and judge anymore; so as to judge everything by love, which is infinite.

Grace was no longer entirely with God; it was given to man. Not only shown to the sinner from afar, but also given to him as his own—in such a way that my sins and God's love are not merely opposed but so that my human love receives a fullness, a greatness, and a value through Christ that are rounded off in grace. So that my love is not a vanishing, creaturely point but something constant and fulfilled. Without Christ, I am only a sinner before God. With Christ, I am, in the eyes of God, a sinner loved by Christ; God sees in me the love that Christ has given me. This love, in which he loves me personally and dies for me, does not remain with him but gives me, a sinner, color and relief in the eyes of God, makes me the brother of his Son, stamps me as a Christian so that God sees in me his Son's love.

And, what is more, apart from the sacraments, for the Son is not merged in them; and though the Father sees us in the light of the sacraments, he does not see the Son through the sacraments. I become a mirror of the Lord's love; I am never again alone before God with my sins. And however much I may struggle against being a Christian, though I protest against being a Christian and will have nothing to do with God—still, God has loved me first, and his irrevocable sign is upon me.

But precisely because they go so deep and take so firm a hold, the signs of grace are also an obligation. Baptism is not only a right and a claim but also an increased obligation. The Lord's grace is given me for my own, a grace for sin and redemption. In baptism, I am called upon to atone with him, because the Lord has atoned for me. The Lord's atonement and the atonement that is required of me are not unconnected. If the Lord in his guiltlessness has expiated my guilt, how much more must I, who am guilty, atone with my Redeemer, even though my expiation, more closely considered, is only a manner of speech. And, in the same way, the grace given me demands that I should be open to God, which means confession.

It is only through grace that confession becomes an act of disclosure, and it is only in the light of grace that I see what I am and what I would be without the grace of God.

Then confession becomes an act of redemption in which my sin is taken away by God more readily than it is shown and offered by man to God. And, finally, in Communion, the grace of God is given to us for our own in such a way that the flesh and blood of the Lord passes into our spirit and our flesh, so that when the Father sees us, he cannot do otherwise than see us in possession of the grace of his Son.

There was also *truth* in the Old Covenant. For there, too, God spoke the truth. But it was a truth adapted to man, a commensurable truth. That is why men thought they could make sure of it in the form of "wisdom". The truth of Christ, on the contrary, is incommensurable, for it is boundless. The essence of truth like the essence of grace altered in passing from the Old to the New Covenant.

Formerly, the truth could be grasped in certain proportions, doctrines, dogmas, rites; it was tied to a visible reality. Its parts could be joined together to form a significant, coherent body in which each part of the truth had its place and fulfilled its function. The parts were finite and coherent; the whole could be seen as a whole, more or less. Each one of God's words had its prescribed meaning, and the various aspects of truth were complementary to one another. But since Christ brought us the truth, since the infinite Word of God was made flesh, the truth is no longer finite and divisible, for each individual Word of God contains the fullness in truth. From now on, it no longer matters whether the Lord speaks at length or briefly, whether he speaks or remains silent, whether we understand much or little. All that is not very important. For the Word of God was made flesh and dwelt among us.

The infinite Word of love has really sounded. From now on, love is the only word in the world, and all other words, all other propositions, all other meanings, are only an expression and a vessel for that one Word. Every finite word gives out the sound of the infinite Word of love.

Nevertheless, the eternal truth speaks in our language and uses human concepts. This entry of the infinite content into the finite container is the reason for the apparently paradoxical character of the Lord's words. Approached with the standards of logic and philosophy, they become a series of riddles and apparent contradictions, unless of course they are modified and the profound mysteries they express are reduced to some moral truth or other and turned into a commonplace. This comes from the fact that we try to measure the infinite with our standards instead of allowing our finite selves to be measured by it. Our standards break to pieces on God because his truth is absolute and all-embracing.

Human logic builds up a system of known and clearly understood propositions; it is the art of excluding everything unknown and unproven from within a limited truth and of introducing clarity and evidence of a sort into a fenced-in enclosure. It is concerned with a completely closed sphere of truth, where there is no place for the unproven, that is, for anything we cannot measure. Logical truth is a concluding truth, a finite truth, whereas the Lord's truth is explosive; it opens the way and draws us progressively into the explosive truth. Human truth is always presented in the form of a series, of a chain; it is consequential. Touched by divine truth, the whole chain breaks at once, or else each individual link is burst open by the explosion. The paradoxical character of the Lord's words is due to that explosive element being introduced into the form of human logic, because the divine truth appeared in human dress. Human truth is finite and is consequently always bounded by another proposition, by its contrary. Divine truth, in contrast, is infinite; it cannot therefore be bounded by anything, not even by its contrary. It therefore contains its opposite when in the form of a human statement, and that element in it must never be weakened, explained away, or disregarded.

The administrator of divine truth is the Bride of the Lord, the Church. When she speaks in the name and with the authority of the Lord, she takes all human thought forms and logic prisoner and is empowered to explode them in the name of God. The truth of God cannot be measured by the evidence of human truth and insight, and, similarly, human evidence cannot be used as a court of appeal against the truth proclaimed by the Church. It must, on the contrary, submit to the all-embracing evidence of divine truth, which is alive in the Church. For just as the Christian no longer lives, but Christ lives in him, so, too, he no longer thinks, except he allows Christ's thought to live in him.

1:18. *No one has ever seen God; the only-begotten Son, who is in the bosom of the Father, he has made him known.*

To see God means to love him so that one can grasp his love. For God is love, and no one sees God except those who love him. To see God therefore means to be so completely in God and his love that nothing except his love matters to us, concerns us, or moves us. So that in everything that happens to us, concerns us, touches us, we allow ourselves to be moved only by his love. To gaze upon him with loving eyes is quite beside the point, for God is Spirit; we must look at him with the love that makes us see.

This is even true of love between people. If I love you and want to explain to a friend who you are and what you mean to me, I am obliged to tell him about your physical and spiritual characteristics; I should try to describe you as I see you in my love. But if there is no love in him, even the most affectionate picture I could paint would leave him cold. If, in contrast, he loves me, then the picture of you I sketched for him will at least awaken in him a desire to know you. His love for me will arouse something in him that is a possible love for you. At first he will see only a rough sum of separate human qualities. If he feels drawn to go farther, he may perhaps begin to draw comparisons; he will discover the qualities that I have described among other people known to him, and he can compare them in order to allow your portrait to come alive.

But there comes a moment when all these means fail. There is a final mysterious, unapproachable residue. Something infinite that defies description. Something that can be reached only in love itself. And, what is more, in a love that possesses the key to that heavenly door behind which your final secret, your original image, your word, is deposited in God. The only approach to this mystery of yours is through faith in God and through love of God. It is only in God that people can really love one another. There is something in you—and it is this that constitutes the very core of your being, what is lovable in you—that comes from God and makes you into a vessel of God's mystery. Whereas all your other qualities and characteristics, being exchangeable, are a matter of indifference, there is a magic about this one element that makes you infinitely lovable in God. That magic, which I can discover only in love, is one with the love with which God loves you. All your other merits are as nothing compared with that love; it is your essence, it is what you are, and it comes from and is God. A friend who knows only the human aspect will want to get to know your essential being more and more closely by studying your characteristics; but the more accurate his study, the farther he gets from your true image, and he ends by gathering together lifeless bricks and mortar. At the very most, he will make of you only what he is capable of imagining. He will construct an image of you instead of contemplating you. He can see you only if he has the key, which is the love of God.

Since the love of God is the key to seeing one's neighbor, it might be thought that perhaps the key could be used only in the case of other Christians. For I know that as a Christian I can embrace and enfold and enclose my co-Christians in the Spirit of God; I have direct access to them. But, in fact, nothing prevents me from including the non-Christian and the anti-Christian in the same love of God, for what comes from God in him is infinitely greater and more essential than that which comes from him. Moreover, although I can embrace a Christian more easily and quickly in my love, because love shines through him, he is less limited and consequently less easy to take in at a glance than the non-Christian. In the case of non-Christians, one can pass quickly through all the spheres that lie fallow, whereas in the Christian they are alive and fruitful. Where Christians are concerned, there is always the possibility of going to the heart of things and digging out the essential, but only because they are richer, more differentiated than non-Christians. One touches on vital matters more quickly because they themselves are more alive. As a Christian, a man is open and expansive toward me, because he is so to God, whereas the non-Christian is reserved, drawn together, bent over himself. Everything in a Christian has direction, a movement toward God. And if I look in that direction, I am led toward his original image in God. And accomplishing with him the movement of his inmost love, I learn to know him as he should be in God.

We can therefore grasp our neighbor, contemplating him within the love of God, and can do so formlessly, at least, in this world. By the grace of God, we can see our neighbor through love, though we cannot see God in this world. We cannot see God because our love is not perfect. One can see one's neighbor imperfectly. But God, who is perfect, cannot be seen by one who is imperfect. Even the purity that is ours after confession is not pure enough for that. For our want of love is something more than our particular, forgivable sins. Our love is not entirely devoted to the love of God. To see God is something indivisible, and once one has seen God, one can no longer take one's gaze off him. And fundamentally we have no wish to see God now, because we know in our heart of hearts that we must first of all finish with our sins. Here below we cannot love perfectly, and the vision of God presupposes perfect love. No man, therefore, has seen God. The contemplation and vision that occur in and through love are only a beginning, a hint of what is promised: to see God in love. In our common love for one another there is a hint, a foreboding of the mystery of God's infinity, the full affirmation of which would be the vision of God.

The only-begotten Son ... has made him known. He is the only Son: the parting of Father and Son is unique and unrepeatable. Once it is consummated, only one thing can follow, infinite dispersal, the Eucharist. He is the only-begotten Son, and we follow immediately after, we who are so numerous as to be innumerable and yet the numbered sons of God. There is no sort of connection between the first and the second parting; the first is unique, the second unending. If the first were vertical, the second would be horizontal. The Son makes the Father known because he is the Father's gift of communication. From the moment he comes on earth, he is the Eucharist. He was the Eucharist since the beginning of the world in the light of his willingness and of his mission. He comes into the world, not in order to depart, but in order to expend himself among us. He comes as one who is love; he unites in himself the Father's love for the world through him and our love, which goes through him to the Father; he is the center between God and us. That is why he is love, for love is always the center. It is the center just as light is the center from which the rays of light radiate. That does not hinder the fact that all light comes from the Father, for the Son is the absolute center; he is the Word in the beginning, in the bosom of the Father. The Father is the light, and love is the radiation, and the only way in which we can be struck by his love is by being innumerable. Just as the Lord in the Eucharist makes himself innumerable so as to become one, we too must be innumerable in order to become one again—in the Lord. In our multiplicity, the unity of the Lord is merged in his love so that our multiplicity may be reduced to the unity of love. It is only in that unity that we can see him—and the Father in him.

The Eucharist represents the quantitative extreme of love, and every Host is of equal value. It contains the same love of man—whether man is worthy or not, good or bad, whether he receives Communion with or without love, or even if he communicates sacrilegiously. The Lord's love strikes upon us all, whatever our state of preparedness. And having thus moved us, he recognizes our thanks— humanly speaking, so very variable—as a sign of love. In that way, he reveals the Father, who allows the sun to shine upon the just and the unjust. He does not choose or elect or select: he spends his love regardless and loves without preference. It is the Son who forces the Father to show no preference. But for the Son, love would also be the law of justice. The Son outshines the law and becomes the law of love; the law was dissolved in love.

But the Son can be known because he was in the Word and because we have acknowledged his Incarnation. He forms the bridge between seeing our neighbor, a duty incumbent upon us, and seeing God, which is impossible. And then again the apostle John forms the bridge between us and the Son, through his entirely human, friendly love for the Lord. One should not scorn genuine human friendship as a way to God and certainly not set up an antithesis between the love of one's friends and love of one's neighbor. For since we are human, living in a human framework, Christian love itself unfolds gradually, starting from friendship. John, as the friend of the Lord, is the mediator of love, the original model and image of each and every one who leads us to the love of the Lord. He gives us a description of the Lord in which we see him up close and human; his love for the Lord shines in his description and reveals the love of the Lord himself. In this, John is the archetype of the priest who leads us to God, just as the Lord is the archetype of the Father's love. Since the Father's love could be revealed only by the love of Christ—and not by his teaching only—we are given John, the beloved disciple, who reveals the Lord's love through his own love.